YOUR FUTURE JOB

BUILDING A CAREER IN THE NEW NORMAL

Your Future Job: Building A Career In The New Normal
Copyright © 2015 Plattekill Press
    P.O. Box 465
    Modena, NY 12548

ISBN 978-0-9963305-0-3 paperback
ISBN 978-0-9963305-1-0 e-book
Library of Congress Control Number: 2015941008
Cataloging-in-Publication Data
    Jelski, Daniel, 1951 -
    George, Thomas F. 1947 -
    Your Future Job: Building A Career In The New Normal
    Daniel Jelski & Thomas F. George
    Cataloging Keywords: Careers for College Students; Careers for High
    School Students; The New Normal in Economics; Choosing a College
    Major; The Gig Economy

Edited by Bob Rich, Ph.D.
bobswriting.com/editing.html
Design by Adam Robinson

YOUR FUTURE JOB

BUILDING A CAREER IN THE NEW NORMAL

Daniel Jelski and Thomas F. George

Plattekill Press

CONTENTS

INTRODUCTION

The world changed in 2008.

To see how, consider the chart in Figure 1. It shows the gross domestic product (GDP) from 2004 through 2013. The GDP is a rough measure of how big the economy is, and growth in GDP usually means growth in the number of jobs, payrolls, wealth, etc. A growing GDP is a good thing.

The black line represents the actual GDP as measured by the Bureau of Economic Analysis, a federal agency. It goes up until 2008 when the Great Recession happened. Indeed, the definition of a recession is when GDP goes down. We definitely had a recession from 2008 until 2009, and a bad one at that.

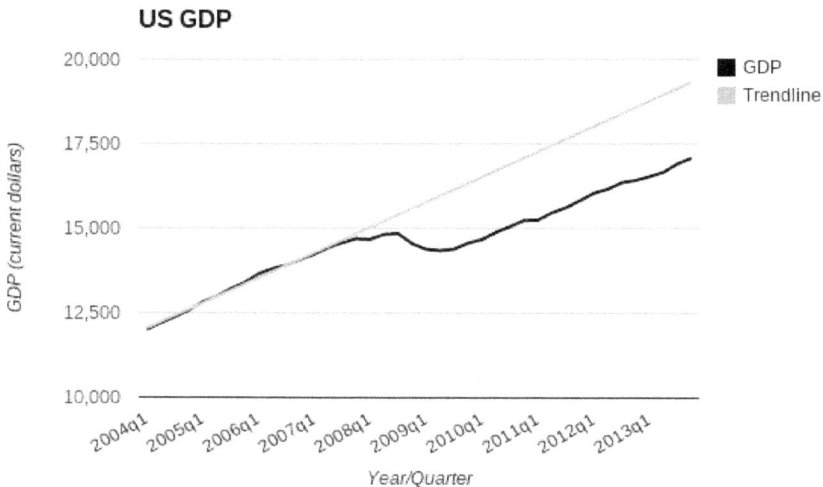

Figure 1: GDP from 2004 through 2013[1]

But that's not the worst of it. Recessions occur all the time, though we usually pull out of them and continue on as before. That didn't happen in 2009. This can be seen by looking at the gray line in Figure 1. That is what we would have expected if the trend in GDP from 2004 through 2007 is extended (*extrapolated* is the technical term) to the present. We can call the gray line the *trendline*. If there hadn't been a recession, then following the trendline, our current GDP would be over $19 trillion rather than the paltry $17 trillion we have today.

Most recessions are followed by a *recovery*. During the recovery, GDP grows faster than normal until it gets back to the trendline, and then the economy goes on its merry way. If we'd had a proper recovery in 2009, GDP would have grown very quickly in 2009 and 2010 until we got back to the trendline. The problem with the 2008 recession is that we never had a proper recovery — we have never gotten back to the trendline. Indeed, even worse, it looks as if the new trendline starting at 2010 is even slower than what it was before.

There has been much debate among economists, political leaders, and the general public as to why things are so bad. Many people think that the recession never ended. It sure seems that way when one looks at the job market, but the consistent GDP growth since 2009 shows that not to be true. The well known economist Tyler Cowen refers to the lag as *The Great Stagnation* — he wrote a book about it with that title[2]. The Federal Reserve, the president, Congress, and lots of other people have worked mightily to fix this problem. Terms like *stimulus*, *quantitative easing*, and *austerity* have all entered the common lexicon, albeit with no apparent effect on the economy.

In this book, we choose to describe the post-recession economy as the *New Normal*. We prefer this term partly because it is *value-neutral*. That is, it does not assume that everything is bad. Obviously there is a lot of bad economic news, but just under the surface there is much good as well.

To see why, consider some ideas from the economist, Joseph Schumpeter (1883-1950). He is famous for the phrase *creative destruction*. In a rapidly changing world (or *dynamic economy*), new technology will render old industries obsolete. For example, the Internet (specifically, *Craigslist*) has mostly destroyed the print newspaper. If you're a newspaper reporter, that's a really bad thing, but for almost everybody else it's a very good thing—*Craigslist* is much cheaper and more convenient than the old-fashioned classified ads.

When you look at the GDP data in Figure 1, you see only the destruction half of *creative destruction*. Newspapers have shed far more jobs than *Craigslist* has created. Further, *Craigslist* is (mostly) free, and so contributes almost nothing to GDP. In that sense, GDP is a poor measure of economic wellbeing, because very few people think we're actually worse off because of *Craigslist*.

The daily headlines mostly talk about the *destruction*, namely all the laid-off newspaper reporters. But your future depends on *creation*—the other half of Schumpeter's equation. And there is a vast amount of creation out there—you just have to know where to look for it. That's why we are very optimistic about the future. Or, put another way, we are very optimistic about <u>your</u> future.

The second reason we like the term *New Normal* is because it implies that things are never going to be the way they used to be—there really is too much destruction going on. The technical term you may hear is that since 2008 there has been a *structural change* in the economy. There will never be a recovery in the sense that we'll get back to the same old trendline—the old days are gone for good. But the economy will, over time, create a new trendline, and we believe that path will lead to much greater prosperity and opportunity.

That's not to say that adjusting to the New Normal will be easy. First is the problem of figuring out precisely what it is.

Since that involves predicting the future, nobody really knows for sure, but we're going to give it a good try.

Second, you need to adjust your goals and lifestyle to enable a career in the New Normal. Some things you might like to have done may not be possible anymore. On the other hand, fresh opportunities await. The advice you get from your parents and teachers—who lived in the olden days—may not always be relevant.

And finally, you will be forced to take risks. The future is more uncertain than ever, and some things you think are good ideas today will not turn out very well later on. That happens to everybody (though more likely to you), and there's nothing you can do about that. But you need to anticipate and *hedge* those risks as much as possible. *Hedge* means to have a Plan B, an alternative that lets you out with as small a loss as possible.

This book will guide you through the jungle. It is an educated guess as to what the New Normal will look like, along with practical advice on how you can best prepare yourself for a future career.

Your authors are Dan Jelski and Tom George. Dan is a chemistry professor at a state college, nearing retirement. He has lots of experience looking for jobs, and has counseled many, many students about careers. He formerly served as a campus administrator, responsible for hiring people—he's sat on both sides of the job-interview table. Further, his abiding avocation is economics, and he has studied things like labor markets and recessions.

Tom is the president of a large, urban, state university, with a birdseye view of how a college education feeds into the economy. He has extensive personal experience in the interview process for new jobs during his move up the academic ranks. Neither of us has settled only for the security of being a tenured professor.

The views expressed here are entirely our own, and do not represent either our institutions or our professions. We're talking outside of school. Indeed, Dan and Tom don't necessarily agree on everything between themselves. As the lead author of this book, Dan takes sole responsibility for its content.

This book is not for everybody. For example, if you just graduated from Stanford with an engineering degree, and have already founded your own startup in Silicon Valley, please stop reading now. You don't need our advice.

At the other extreme, Dan has a neighbor, a widow whose son is in his early thirties. The son has never had a job, and is today completely unemployable. You probably all know people like that—unambitious, or who have issues that somehow take them out of economic life.

Instead, this book is intended for people like those who sit in Dan's college classroom or attend Tom's university—people like you. You are people with ambition and talent. You are willing to work hard and make an investment in a better life, for yourself, for your family and children, and for your neighbors.

Our goal is to help you make that investment wisely.

WHAT IS A JOB?

So what do you want to be when you grow up?

President?

An astronaut?

A movie star?

When Dan's son was three or four years old, he had his heart set on being a garbage truck driver.

In centuries past, most people were farmers. If you were the son or daughter of a farmer, then you would grow up to be either a farmer or a farmer's wife. There wasn't much point in worrying about it. Nobody ever asked, "What do you want to be when you grow up?"

By 1700, people began to have some choices—not all of them good—immortalized by the nursery rhyme:

> *Tinker, Tailor*
>
> *Soldier, Sailor*
>
> *Rich man, Poor man*
>
> *Beggarman, Thief*

Today, of course, there are thousands and thousands of different job titles. A precocious four-year-old today might say, "I'd like to be the database administrator for a large, urban hospital, running Oracle software." The reason we have so many job titles today is because we're so much richer.

Supply Chains

Actually, it's the other way round. As the Scottish economist Adam Smith (1723-1790) pointed out, societies get richer as jobs become more and more specialized. We can illustrate this by example.

Farmer Bob goes to Farmer Bill and says, "Hey, Bill—I'll give you my tomato for your potato." And maybe they'll make the trade, but it doesn't really accomplish very much. After all, both Bob and Bill can grow both tomatoes and potatoes, so there's really no point in trading. They can help each other out—Amish farmers famously help each other build barns. But if all your neighbors are farmers, then there isn't very much to trade, and it's a subsistence level, *eat what you grow* economy.

Now suppose Doc Charles moves to the area. Farmer Bob has taken ill and says to the doctor "I'll give you some tomatoes if you can cure my ailment." Now that's a real trade—Doc Charles gets fresh tomatoes, and Farmer Bob feels better.

Doc Charles scribbles down a few notes about Bob's ailment, hoping he doesn't forget. But he gets pretty busy with all the other farmers in the area, and then he can't remember if Bob had a knee sickness or an elbow sickness. So he hires Mary to transcribe his notes for him and keep them organized.

That works for awhile, but soon enough there are a lot of other doctors in town. There's the knee doctor and the elbow doctor, the nose doctor and the eye doctor, and there's even the head doctor who becomes known as the shrink. Mary can't keep up anymore, so they hire Jennifer, who administers the Oracle database storing medical records at the large hospital in a nearby city.

Whenever Farmer Bob gets sick, he makes sure to give Jennifer a few tomatoes. Not directly, of course—it's all mediated by money. Bob has likely never met Jennifer and probably doesn't even know what an Oracle database is. Still, precisely because they do such different things, the trade is highly valuable to both Bob and Jennifer. He gets much better medical care from a whole army of doctors, and Jennifer gets fresh tomatoes.

Tomatoes and health care—that's what it's all about. In order to provide Bob with better health care, this whole complicated *supply chain* developed—doctors, nurses, databases, syringes and needles, pharmaceuticals, computers, linens, soap, disinfectants, etc., etc., etc. Thousands and thousands of people work hard every day to provide Bob (and people like him) with good medical care.

And why do they do it? Because they want fresh tomatoes. Of course, Bob doesn't produce tomatoes by himself. He is also part of a very complicated supply chain: fertilizers, pesticides, tractors, seeds, refrigeration, transport, packaging, retailing, etc. Again, thousands of people are working hard every day just so that Jennifer (and people like her) can have fresh tomatoes.

Consumer Benefit

Put more generally, Bob's supply chain is trading tomatoes in exchange for the medical care produced by Jennifer's supply chain. They all work hard for one reason: Bob's people want medical care, and Jennifer's people want tomatoes. The medical care and the tomatoes are known as the *consumer benefit*.

Consumer benefit is the net benefit that consumers get from buying your product. Farmer Bob can sell tomatoes only because Jennifer enjoys eating them. Farmer Bob's goal is to create consumer benefit, from which he can capture a profit that enables him to buy the consumer benefit created by Jennifer's supply chain.

Consumer benefit is what makes the economy go round. It is very hard to measure directly—that's why people measure GDP instead. GDP and consumer benefit are similar but not the same thing. Some things, such as *Craigslist* or *Google*, contribute huge consumer benefit, but only a little bit to GDP. Others, such as the military or prisons, do not contribute to consumer benefit, but make up a significant part of GDP. These are expenses society incurs because of the failings of human nature.

The economy consists of a large number of supply chains, each of which produces consumer items that they trade with each other.

So, gentle reader, if you are still with us, you are a very industrious and diligent student who will undoubtedly have a successful career. But now it's time to cash in—we promised to tell you what a job is.

Jobs, Supply Chains and Specialization

A job is a step in a supply chain (or chains) that produces consumer benefit.

When you are looking for a job or a career, there are several questions you should ask.

- What is the consumer product your supply chain will ultimately produce? Is it medical care, agricultural produce, entertainment, transportation? Will consumers buy it? Will they still be buying it twenty years from now?

- How valuable is the consumer product you will be making? You will earn more money in a high-value market than a low-value one. Medical care is more expensive than tomatoes, which in turn is more valuable than pet rocks.

- How long and complicated is the supply chain? Generally, expensive products (such as automobiles) have very long supply chains that span the globe, while vegetable produce tends to be more local. The longer the supply chain, the more valuable the product, but the more susceptible your job will be to technological or economic disruption.

- What is your role in the supply chain? A farmer plays a central role in food production and is unlikely to ever be completely unemployed. Dan is a chemistry professor, and so plays a tangential role in medical and engineering professions, along with whatever supply chains they might be part of. But the role is so slight that employment as a chemistry professor is probably much less secure.

Some examples may illustrate.

Many students major in computer science, including our fictitious database administrator, Jennifer. But computer science is not a consumer product—when was the last time your parents brought some computer science home for dinner? Instead, computer science is a remarkably flexible *tool* that can be used in any number of supply chains. Jennifer uses that tool to provide medical services to consumers. *Her income comes from medical services, not from computer science.*

As she advances in her career, her expertise will become increasingly specialized within the medical industry. As previously described, specialization makes us richer, and in particular it will make Jennifer richer. That is until technological change renders the job of medical database administrator obsolete. At some point Jennifer may be too specialized to easily shift careers into some other supply chain. She may end up unemployed.

Dan's daughter majored in English. She didn't aspire to become an Englishwoman, or an English teacher, or even an English professor. Instead, her education, interest in writing, and good fortune led her to become a journalist for a trade magazine. Analogous to Jennifer, writing is a tool. *Her income comes from the trade she writes about, not from her English degree.* She's part of the supply chain whose product you consume whenever you tip back a glass of beer or open a bottle of wine. Cheers!

This is why the question *What are you going to do with an English degree?* is so nonsensical. Dan's daughter sells booze with her English degree—who woulda thunk? Like computer science, English is a very flexible tool that will fit into any number of different supply chains. Some college majors are similarly flexible: political science, philosophy, mathematics. Others are much more limiting: hospitality management, engineering, medicine.

There is a trade-off between specialization and flexibility. English is probably a more flexible major than computer science—Dan's daughter, by virtue of being less specialized, will have an easier time shifting to a new supply chain than Jennifer. By the same token, his daughter doesn't earn so much. The extra salary that Jennifer earns can be thought of as a risk premium. She adds more value because of her technical specialty, but she's at much greater risk of future unemployment. Dan's daughter is unlikely ever to be unemployed.

Some jobs seem like sure things today, but they probably aren't. Medical doctors have many years of education and training, and are in highly specialized fields. Accordingly, they earn high salaries. What is often not realized is how susceptible that profession is to technological disruption—in our view, medicine is a very high-risk profession precisely because it is so specialized.

You may have heard of IBM's *Watson* computer, the one that became the *Jeopardy* champion. IBM didn't build that computer just to play *Jeopardy*, but rather to make medical diagnoses. Indeed, *Watson* now turns out to be better at diagnosing cancer than most humans.[3] We only hope those humans are current on their unemployment insurance premiums!

So you have a choice. You can major in a very specialized subject like medicine or engineering (or specialize in a particular application of computer science). You will earn a higher salary, but you may also be at much greater risk of unemployment later in life. Or you can major in something more generic and flexible, like English or philosophy. Your starting salary will be a lot lower, but your ability to move within and between supply chains will be greater. You're less likely to be unemployed.

There is a second choice you have to make. Should you major in a *tool*, such as English or computer science, or in a *supply chain*, such as medicine, education, or hospitality management? The latter is preparation for a job in a specific industry, but locks you into it right away. Your future career will depend entirely on the economic fortunes of the consumer good that supply chain produces—imagine if you'd studied newspaper reporting. Studying a tool, on the other hand, is much more flexible. But because you are less specialized, you will earn substantially less on your first job, and you may have a hard time finding that first job. Either way, at some point you are going to have to decide what supply chain you want to attach yourself to. That's the really important decision, because that's going to determine how you earn your money for your career.

In the last chapter, we discussed hedging your risks. If you are risk averse, we suggest you study a tool, such as math or English. If, on the other hand, you're really passionate about a particular topic and willing to put it all on the line, then by all means go for a supply chain, like medicine or engineering. Other disciplines, such as chemistry or business, hang somewhere in the middle between those two poles.

Case Study: Social Media

An employment agency called *The Creative Group* (TCG) hosts a superb webpage with lots of information about social media jobs.[4] This includes position descriptions and even salary ranges. Let's look at some of that information using the tools we've developed in this chapter, beginning with the four key questions.

What is the ultimate consumer product your supply chain will produce? Social media is a form of advertising that is most useful for what is known as the *consumer discretionary market*. These are items that people enjoy buying, but don't consider necessities. It includes things like restaurants, gourmet food and drink, fashion and cosmetics, vacation travel, and home decor. By contrast, few people consult social media when buying groceries, car tires, gasoline, or workaday clothing.

Consumer discretionary is definitely a durable market and will be around for a very long time. However, it is not a rapidly growing one—and is definitely hurt by the decline in GDP. Further, growth depends on population growth, which is slowing. On the other hand, growth in emerging markets such as China and India increases the number of people who buy things for fun.

How valuable is the consumer product you will be making? Most people don't have a lot of money for discretionary items. Yes, there are a few people who can spring for a Mercedes or a Ferrari on a lark, but most are content with going out to eat once or twice a week. So, this tends to be a low-value market.

How long and complicated is the supply chain? Defining supply chains is usually pretty ambiguous, and where you draw the line is a bit arbitrary. Restaurants, for example, depend on the entire agriculture industry, and that supply chain is incredibly long. But let's restrict our attention to the part that makes it *discretionary*, i.e., the part that is specific to restaurants. So the local farmer's market selling fresh produce is part of the supply chain, but the large food processing plant in the Midwest is not. With this caveat, the supply chain is relatively short, consistent with the fact that discretionary items are relatively low-value.

What is your role in the supply chain? Social media people are a core part of the consumer discretionary supply chain. By definition, these are things that consumers do not have to buy, and hence advertising is extremely important. The cynic will say you are trying to talk people into buying things they neither need nor want. Our view is more generous: you are giving people an opportunity to have fun. Either way, your career is most secure when the people who buy your product enjoy using it.

Bottom line: Consumer discretionary is a very durable market that will make for a successful career over the long term. It depends crucially on advertising, of which social media is an important part. However, the product is of relatively low value, and the industry looks to grow slowly. Therefore, you won't get rich.

So what's with this highfalutin *social media* term? In part, it's just employment agency hype—they are trying to convince their customers (employers) that their people have some special, rare talent. Accordingly, they greatly exaggerate how difficult it is to find people—looking at the TCG webpage you'd think there was a huge shortage of social media professionals. Almost always, you can't trust employers' descriptions of the labor market—they always think there's a shortage. On the other hand, social media does represent a new employment opportunity—what used to be advertised on the radio now shows up on *Facebook*.

TCG provides a long list of job descriptions.[5] Let's look at three of them and see how they fit into the ideas of this chapter.

A <u>blogger</u> is "responsible for opinionated, stylish writing and frequently posting new content to the internet." The key requirement is "must demonstrate an ability to write professionally for varied audiences and meet tight deadlines."

A blogger's job is really about good writing, something that was important long before there was social media, and will be necessary long after the social media fad has faded. Somebody who can write well will always have a job. But this is not a specialized position—the salary is relatively low. Their salary guide[6] (Creative Group 2015) quotes a range from $43K to $65K.

An <u>interactive project manager</u> requires "a demonstrable knowledge of Internet protocols such as HTML, Javascript, XML, web publishing, and database structure. Experience with Microsoft Project, Visio, and Excel is preferred."

This is a highly specialized, technical job. It did not exist ten years ago, and it likely will not exist ten years from now. Consistent with our above analysis, we would expect a significant risk premium, and hence higher pay. We can't find that specific job title in the salary guide, but an *interactive producer* earns between $73K and $103K.

Finally, consider a leadership position, such as a <u>director of social media</u>. This person is "responsible for developing and overseeing the execution of strategic social media and digital initiatives, including developing and managing viral marketing campaigns, creating and supervising high-profile channel accounts, and integrating interactive media into the overall business strategy." The quoted salary (as best we can determine) is between $100K and $135K.

Study Questions

Compare a computer science major and an English major, both starting out in social media careers. Give reasons for your answers.

1. Who will earn the highest initial salary?

2. Who will have an easier time finding the first job?

3. Who will learn more about the consumer discretionary market?

4. Who has the greater job security? What could the other person do to increase job security?

5. Who is more likely to move into a management position? What could the other person do to create a better path to management?

WHAT'S NEW ABOUT NORMAL?

The Great Recession of 2008 is named after the Great Depression from 1929 to 1939. The latter was a worldwide economic downturn. To better understand the Great Recession, it's useful to back up and think about that earlier event. It's effect on the US is shown by the shaded part in Figure 2.

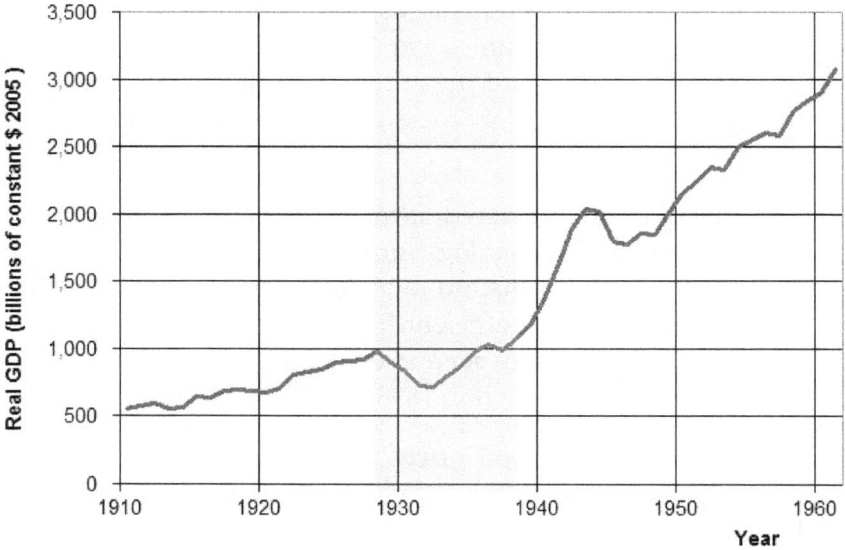

Figure 2: US GDP from 1910 to 1962[7]

There are many possible explanations for the Great Depression, but the view most useful for us is presented by Arnold Kling.[8]

Most high school students have read *The Grapes of Wrath* by John Steinbeck.[9] If you haven't read it, do so—it's a wonderful book. It vividly describes how small-time farmers went bankrupt and were forced off the land when the banks evicted them. The immediate cause of the disaster was the dust bowl in the 1930s—there were no crops some years. The farmers couldn't make good on their debts.

But the real problem began many years earlier (in the 1880s) with inventions by two men. A German, Gottlieb Daimler (1834-1900), invented the internal combustion engine. And an American (born in Serbia) named Nikola Tesla (1856-1943) invented the electric motor (among many other things).

For a few years, these were toys. Some states passed "red flag laws," requiring a man with a red flag to walk in front of any "horseless carriage." An electric motor without a ready source of electric power was equally useless. But, slowly, the inventions moved mainstream. Ford Motor Company introduced the Model T in 1908 and the automobile age began, though it took until the 1950s before there were decent roads for them to drive on.

The first gasoline-powered farm tractor was built in Iowa in 1892, and the technology gradually improved. Gasoline engines improved transportation for farm products, making marketing much more efficient. The spread of electricity made grain milling much cheaper and enabled baking in large factories. *Nabisco* was founded in 1898.

The result was that food prices went down. Because of new technology, you got more consumer benefit food for your labor and investment. Consumers did very well.

But not everybody benefited. Buying a newfangled tractor cost money, and it couldn't pay for itself if you didn't have a big enough farm. So the small farmers in Oklahoma were squeezed both ways. The prices they got for their product went down, and they had no ability to mechanize their farms. Every Spring they'd borrow money to plant their crop, and then never be able to fully pay it back after the harvest. Each year they went deeper in debt. The dust bowl was the final straw.

Before the depression, Farmer Bob, Farmer Bill, and Steinbeck's hero, Tom Joad, could eke out a living in semi-subsistence agriculture. After the depression that became impossible. In the 1870s, approximately 75% of all Americans worked in agriculture. Today, it's less than 2%.

The mechanization of agriculture hugely improved the consumer benefit. Consumers got more and better food for less money. But it also disrupted the lives of people who worked in agriculture. For a decade or two they could ignore the new technology. For another decade they could pretend it would go away, muddling through by taking out loans.

But eventually the old way of life became impossible. Some precipitating event—the dust bowl, or the stock market crash, or the popping of the housing bubble—finally ends the old economy. It's like an earthquake. Pressure builds beneath the surface for many years. Nobody notices. Or they pretend not to notice. But eventually some event—trivial in itself—causes a sudden shift. The ground moves, never to return to where it used to be.

We suggest that events like the Great Depression and the Great Recession are ultimately caused by new technology. The gasoline engine and the electric motor were the root causes of the Great Depression. What technology caused the Great Recession?

Computer Technology

The answer is computers, or more generally, *digital technology*. This term includes the Internet, mobile telephony, fiber optics, and all the other digital gizmos that now improve our lives. With this in mind, the parallels between the Great Depression and the Great Recession are uncanny. Here are some representative events.

- 1947 - John Bardeen, Walter Brattain, and William Shockley invent the solid state transistor.
- 1964 - IBM markets the successful computer mainframe, the System 360. This machine influences computer architecture to our present day.
- 1972 - Atari is founded.
- 1977 - The first successful home computer, the Apple II, debuts.
- 1979 - First commercial cellular phone service is launched in Japan.
- 1981 - General Electric produces fiber optic cable up to 25 miles long.
- 1982 - The Internet Protocol Suite (TCP/IP) is standardized. This can be taken as the start date for the Internet.
- 1990 - Tim Berners-Lee completes construction of the first web browser and invents the World Wide Web.
- 1995 - Craigslist is founded.
- 1998 - Google is founded.
- 2001 - Wikipedia is founded.
- 2007 - The iPhone is introduced.

Mirroring the toy-like horseless carriage, games and entertainment figured heavily among the first uses of computers. Indeed, the moon landing in 1969 represented the first major accomplishment of the new technology, but can hardly be thought of as essential to the economy. We went to the moon because it was there, not because we wanted to eat green cheese.

The "killer apps" came with the advent of the personal computer in the 1970s. These were things like word processing, spreadsheets, and some simple-minded database software—stuff we take for granted nowadays. But then it was a big deal—a company called *Wang Laboratories* sold computers that could do nothing besides word processing—and they were big hits.

Today the "killer apps" are all available for free through *Google Docs* and other sources. This book, for example, is being written using *Google Docs*. For approximately $50 it can be translated into a .mobi or .epub document (assuming we don't do that ourselves) and properly formatted to be easily read on your e-reader. It is remarkably easy to publish a book these days.

In 2014 two MIT professors, Erik Brynjolfsson and Andrew McAfee, published *The Second Machine Age*,[10] a book precisely about the effects of digital technology. You've probably heard of Moore's Law, which states that the speed (and related capabilities, such as communications) of computers roughly doubles every 18 months. The U.S. Bureau of Economic Analysis began tracking an investment category called *information technology* back in 1958. Counting that as year zero means that by 2006 computer capabilities had doubled 32 times. That is, computers were 2^{32} = 4,294,967,296 times more powerful in 2006 than they were in 1958.

As of this writing, in 2014, it's been eight years since 2006, which means computer capability has doubled yet another four times. That brings us to a multiple of 68,719,476,736—or nearly 70 billion! Brynjolfsson and McAfee predict this trend will continue, albeit in a different way. Instead of simply redoubling processing speed, for which we've run up against physical limits, we are also able to dramatically improve software. So whatever computers can do now, they'll be able to do much more of it in the future.

Driverless Trucks

Of course, computers can't do things the same way that humans can. For example, it is now possible for a computer to drive a truck (or a car) across the country without human assistance (as long as it stays on or near the Interstate; automated trucks can't quite navigate city traffic yet). Humans can do that because we have good vision—we can read signs that say "Kalamazoo—Next Right." That won't work for computers—computer vision is still very primitive compared to what humans can see. And for that reason, people believed that computers could never drive trucks.

But two things changed. First came GPS. That means the computer knows exactly where it is. And second came comprehensively detailed maps, such as supplied by Google. That means the computer knows what exit to take without having to read any signs. Indeed, every bend in the road is carefully mapped. The computer can navigate without seeing anything.

The truck-driving computer doesn't need to see very much. It only needs to see the lane markers, and it needs to slow down or stop if something in front of it does the same. And here the automated truck has an advantage. It can use cameras on all sides of the truck—there are no blind spots. Further, it can use Lidar technology to determine how fast the car in front is moving—this is already in widespread use in the form of adaptive cruise control. The computer never falls asleep, is always fully attentive, and measures reaction time in milliseconds. It can drive 24 hours per day. The result is that automated trucks are safer, cheaper and faster than the human-driven sort.

It is only a matter of time before automated trucks dominate the nation's highways. The consumer benefit will be huge—costs for things like fresh produce from California will decline dramatically. But millions of jobs will be lost. Over-the-road truck drivers will go the way of Pony Express riders.

And not just truck drivers. Computers, which are primitive today compared to what they'll be ten or twenty years from now, will displace millions of workers in lots of professions. Brynjolfsson and McAfee cite the following table as a guide:

Table 1: Automation by job type

Jobs	Routine	Non-routine
Manual	Already automated	Not easily automated
Cognitive	Being automated now	Not easily automated

Manual routine jobs include a factory assembly-line worker. These jobs are already mostly gone, and the few that remain are disappearing. Similar jobs in fast-food places—flipping burgers—are also on the verge of automation. All of that can be done by machine.

Cognitive routine jobs are being automated right now. Dan's father was a travel agent—a job that mostly doesn't exist anymore. Accountants are increasingly displaced by software, such as *Turbotax*. Routine legal work is being automated—we'll have more to say about that in a minute. Indeed, there is a long list of jobs that are in whole or in part on their way out: secretary, receptionist, purchasing agent, retail clerk, telemarketer, etc. Whole swaths of the pink collar and white collar workforce are on the bubble. Tom Joad knows exactly how they feel.

The non-routine manual jobs are a different story. Because computers continue to have relatively poor eyesight and hearing, and also are not particularly good at walking around (though there is some progress[11]) there are many things they can't do. Home health care aide jobs look to be pretty safe. Even if a computer had good vision, it still couldn't easily talk to patients. A lot of skilled trades fall into this category—plumbers, electricians, carpenters—and it will be a long time before they're displaced by computers.

Here's our prediction: computers will never possess vision, hearing, feel, smell, or taste that in any way rivals that of a human—at least not in your lifetime. We'll change our mind when a robot can play major league baseball or compete in a PGA golf tournament under the same rules as a human being.

Consider vision for example. Human vision does not just depend on the eye, but also on hormones. Human color perception is as much a matter of psychology as of physics. It's a horrendously complicated process that evolved over a billion years (and/or created by God). A computer's digital simulation of human vision will never duplicate the incredibly messy analog reality. Computers are valuable tools that can substantially augment human vision, but they are not even close to replacing us. They can't even read a sign that says "Kalamazoo—Next Right."

We are very much aware of the fact that ten years ago people predicted that computers could never drive a car. But in some ways that's true—computers are nowhere near being able to drive a car the way people do. They simply can't see well enough. Instead, a workaround has been discovered. Likewise, with computerized language translation—the computer doesn't do it the way people do. The computer understands nothing. So, while some skilled trades may be displaced via similar workarounds, most of them won't be. They will remain human jobs.

Computers can flip burgers, but they will never be able to taste food and judge whether or not customers will enjoy it. The skilled chef will always have a job. A computer can diagnose cancer, but only a skilled human being can gather the necessary data from a patient, either by observation or conversation. The primary care physician (or nurse) will always have a job.

Computers can replace the cashier and ring up purchases, but they will never rival the good salesman. If you already know what kind of car you want, you can order it online. But if you're not sure, then the personable car salesman is going to play a role in your decision. Likewise with the real estate agent, or even those travel agents that still exist.

The "Cognitive Elite"

And finally, in the fourth box are the non-routine cognitive jobs, a category that traditionally includes lawyer, professor and doctor. Tyler Cowen refers to them as jobs for the "cognitive elite," by which he means people who can work with computers rather than against them. Certainly these are the jobs that many readers of this book aspire to. Table 1 suggests that these jobs will not be automated.

We don't entirely agree with that conclusion, and that's why we've put that table entry in italics. The category is more complicated than the simple description *non-routine cognitive* implies.

In the last few years, a new word has entered the language: *big data*. This refers to the analysis of a large amount of data, from which conclusions can be drawn. The *Jeopardy*-playing computer, *Watson*, had millions and millions of trivia data stored in its memory, along with an algorithm to retrieve them on command. Its command of *big data* allowed it to beat a human *Jeopardy* player. Computers just memorize all the answers. That's the way they drive a truck—they don't need to see the road because they've memorized it. Computers have a better memory than you do.

Computers can also do math better than you can. *Math* really means any kind of logical manipulation—not just with numbers. They can manipulate words just as easily, and they can do it very quickly. While chess-playing computers have memorized all possible moves for the first 15 or 20 moves into the game, after that they use logic to calculate further moves. As computers get bigger, they'll simply memorize whole games and dispense with the math. Then it will be impossible to take them by surprise.

Here's where the "cognitive elite" are going to run into trouble. Any job that requires a large amount of memorization will be computerized. As mentioned, that includes many doctors.

They spend years in medical school memorizing diseases, symptoms and treatments. This is not time well-spent. Computers will take over that part of the physician's job. Similarly, professors pride themselves as founts of knowledge. Sorry Prof, but computers know more than you do.

So here is what it means for you:

- Your future career depends on *skills* much more than *knowledge*. Roughly put, computers know things, but they can't do things.

- The more *specialized* you are, the more your job is at risk for automation. The *general practitioner* will be employed long after the *oncology specialist* is laid off.

- Jobs that employ the five senses in a sophisticated way are more secure than those that don't. The chef and the artist have secure jobs. The laboratory technician maybe not so much.

- People skills are really important.

And one last point. The jobs most likely to be automated are the ones that save the most money. It's easy to automate hamburger-flipping, but it won't save you a lot of money. Flipping is a low-paid, minimum-wage job, still sufficiently low that the investment in automation is not yet worth it.

But doctors? They get paid a lot, and any part of their job that can be automated goes straight to consumer benefit. That's why big companies like IBM are working very hard to put doctors out of a job. No comparable organization is targeting the lowly hamburger flipper.

So, one more thing to think about: the bigger your paycheck, the bigger the target on your back, and the bigger your risk of unemployment.

Case Study: Lawyers

According to the Wall Street Journal,[12] new enrollment in America's law schools reached a low in 2013, unrivalled since 1977. The precipitous decline began in 2010 as potential students reacted to the similarly large drop in jobs and salaries for lawyers. Growing numbers of newly graduated lawyers can't find jobs, and many of the jobs they do find don't pay very well—certainly not well enough to repay six-figure student loans. Noam Scheiber[13] reports on one young woman who went from earning $200K annually at a Big Law Chicago firm to doing criminal law in small-town Michigan for $40K. That's an 80% pay cut!

The changed circumstances happened very quickly. In 2006 lawyers were doing very well, and law school seemed like an excellent investment. By 2008 the bottom dropped out of the legal market, but most people thought that was temporary response to the recession. Students flooded into law school partly to ride out the recession.

But by 2010 it was clear that things had changed for good. The old days were never coming back. The $500/billable hour business model no longer worked. Many students who had borrowed $100K or more to go to law school will never be able to make good on the investment. The earthquake has arrived.

Are there any lawyers named Tom Joad?

Our model suggests that the housing bubble and the recession did not cause the collapse in lawyer jobs. Instead, new technology and globalization has undermined the old business model for a long time. The recession merely forced the issue.

So what technology reduced the demand for lawyers?

Enron was an electricity trading company that allegedly made money by buying electricity for cheap and selling it for more. But rampant fraud and corruption were revealed beginning in

2001, with the company going bankrupt in 2004. Many Enron executives were sentenced to long prison terms (e.g., Jeffrey Skilling).

Making a case against company executives required going through a huge amount of data, a process that lawyers call *discovery*. In Enron's case, this meant going through 600,000 e-mails among 158 employees, looking for evidence of criminal activity. This was a very arduous, boring job that nevertheless represented entry-level employment for new law graduates.

These 600,000 e-mails are now known as the *Enron Data Set*, and they have become an extremely important dataset for new technology known as *e-discovery*. E-discovery computerizes the discovery process. The *Enron Data Set* is still widely used to teach computers what to look for and how to look for it.

Computers are becoming ever more sophisticated. For example, the computer can look for events when the participants want to move the conversation offline and talk further by phone or in person. This may be evidence of criminal intent. Not even a lawyer could catch that one.

To see how much money this saves, the New York Times[14] reports that in 1978 it cost $2.2 million (presumably in 1978 dollars) to search six million documents. By comparison, in 2011, searching 1.5 million documents cost less than $100,000. That's a huge cost saving. Of course, all that money was saved by not hiring lawyers—no surprise that the market for new grads dried up.

Further, because of improved communications, it is now cheaper to move discovery offshore. Somebody still needs to read the documents the computer identifies, and somebody in India costs less than somebody in the US.

Beyond this, companies that used to hire Big Law firms have learned it's cheaper to do it in-house with a small fraction of the staff. Much routine legal work is easily computerized—few people need that many lawyers anymore. That's why the Big Law firms are shrinking or, in some cases, going bankrupt.

So, highly specialized lawyers are now out of work. In 2006, we can easily imagine parents telling their kids *Go to law school. It's a secure career.* Your parents may have told you the same thing about medical school or engineering. And it might be true. Then again, it might not. There is nothing wrong with being a lawyer, a doctor or an engineer, but you need to have your eyes wide open before you invest in these specialized, knowledge-based careers.

Here's what we can say about lawyers:

- Law is mostly not a consumer good. That means you will (usually) be hired by companies, and they will view you as an expense. In a world where knowledge can be easily computerized, that's not a very good place to be.

- Not everything lawyers do can be automated. We doubt that any robot will ever give closing arguments to a jury in a criminal trial. That will always be a job for humans, albeit probably poorly paid humans.

- Computers can "do" law, but they can't understand the law. They have no clue about the moral, political, and constitutional issues that underlie the profession. Human lawyers will always be at the top of the profession: as politicians, judges, and managers of complex cases.

Neither the law nor anything else is a "safe" career. In the New Normal, anything that can be automated eventually will be.

Study Questions

Consider high school teaching as a career and answer the following questions. Or, if you prefer, substitute in another profession of your choice.

1. What parts of the teacher's job can be automated?

2. What parts of the teacher's job are likely to remain human?

3. How will automation likely change the nature of the profession?

4. If you wanted to be a teacher now, will you still want to be a teacher in the New Normal?

5. What kind of new jobs might be created as a result of teachers being automated?

BE GOOD AT WHAT YOU DO

You've probably gotten contradictory advice. On the one hand, a college admissions officer tells you, "Major in what you love. That's what's most important, and everything else will eventually follow." And then they'll trot out numbers that purport to show that, over the long run, liberal arts majors make as much as engineers.

On the other hand, you've maybe had an uncle, or a neighbor, or even your parents suggest that you should "study something practical, like physical therapy or engineering" (or *law*, we could add just to be funny). Don't do what you love — study something practical.

Author Aaron Clarey wrote a book entitled *Worthless*[15], where he argues against liberal arts majors. For example,

> English has got to be the most worthless degree in the entire English-speaking world. The reason should be blindingly obvious. **YOU ALREADY SPEAK ENGLISH!** If you are 18 years old and got accepted into an accredited college, then it's a pretty safe bet you're fluent enough in English. You can read it, write it, and speak it pretty darn good by now. The only possible reason I can see people choosing English as a major is if they wish to speak it "real good."

We have already established that the so-called "secure professions" are anything but. Specialized jobs are at high risk for automation, globalization, and downsizing, with high-paying jobs most at risk. Your uncle and your neighbor don't know about the New Normal.

Mr. Clarey (who basically argues that everybody should major in engineering) is probably being facetious in his tirade against English. Most college freshmen don't know how to write a coherent paragraph. For that matter, neither do most college graduates. Good writing requires both skill and talent and can't be done by a computer. So there are jobs for English majors—Dan's daughter is a case in point.

Then again, *Do what you love* is terrible advice. Nobody is going to pay you for your hobby. President Obama got himself in trouble recently by criticizing art history. He said[16]

> I promise you folks can make a lot more, potentially, with skilled manufacturing or the trades than they might with an art history degree. Now, nothing wrong with an art history degree—I love art history. So I don't want to get a bunch of e-mails from everybody.

He did get a lot of email from college professors of art history defending the value of their discipline, and he eventually issued an apology. But he was quite right—majoring in art history just because you love it is not a very good idea.

So does that mean nobody should ever major in art history?

Here are three rules for deciding on a career (or, if you're going to college, what to major in):

1. You have to be good at what you do.
2. You need to understand how your proposed career produces consumer benefit, i.e., do the analysis we did in Chapter 2.
3. You shouldn't choose a popular major where the marketplace is likely out of whack.

Let's consider these in order.

How Good Do You Have to be?

How good do you have to be? That depends on the profession.

To take an extreme example, suppose you love playing basketball. It is certainly possible to make a living—indeed, a very good living—as a professional basketball player for the NBA. But in order to do that, you have to be very, very good at basketball. Simply being in love with it is not near enough. Probably fewer than 1% of people who love basketball ever succeed in the NBA. Before you embark on a basketball career, it's important that you have a realistic assessment of your abilities.

For an English major the odds are not quite so bad. Still, probably the majority of English majors are not good enough to work as professional wordsmiths. Dan's daughter earns a living in trade journalism—a perfectly good job that won't be computerized. But despite all the English majors out there, her company has a hard time finding the right people for positions. While the odds are nowhere near as long as playing for the NBA, most applicants are not good enough. The English degree isn't much help for them.

As Bryan Caplan suggests, *If you are doing something hard and not succeeding, then you can either try harder, or do something easier. Often the best choice is to do something easier.*[17] If you are not getting sufficiently good grades in your major, it may very well be you need to change your major. *Change Majors Now.*

Dan had a student who was a biology major. She graduated, probably with a B average. She then spent the better part of a year looking for a job, and finally settled for a position she could've gotten with a high school diploma. Her plan is to go back to school for a nursing license (for which she doesn't need the biology degree). So, unless she can make it pay off for her later, she's wasted four years of her life and lots of money. She should've dropped out or changed majors a long time ago.

Perhaps the most important advice we can give you is to be good at what you do. That means better than most other people in that field. It matters less what career you choose—it is essential that you be good at it, whatever it is.

Invest in a Skill

The second rule will keep you grounded in reality.

The old saw is that it's the philosophy major who tells the engineers what to do. That's the story a lot of professors tell in their defense of the liberal arts. And it has some truth. There is a philosophy major of our acquaintance who is the longtime chief information officer (CIO) for our campus (he's in charge of all the computers). Philosophy is an excellent college major. You will learn how to read very carefully, and to see to the heart of any argument. It's a standard pre-law major, but also is excellent preparation for a technical career.

But you can't just learn philosophy. Philosophy is not a consumer good—nobody is going to buy philosophy. (Becoming a professional philosopher is like playing NBA basketball, except harder.) So, in addition to philosophy, you have to learn a *skill*—a skill (that a computer can't do) relevant to some consumer product that will generate your income.

In order to boss engineers around, you need to know engineering—so along with philosophy, take some engineering classes. Many philosophy students plan on law school, which used to be a more marketable skill than it is today. (Though even today, if you are good enough at it you can make a very good living as a lawyer.) Our acquaintance eventually got a masters degree in computer science—that skill combined with a philosophy degree led to a job in the C-suite.

Philosophy by itself is a worthless degree, but coupled with a marketable skill, it becomes very valuable. It isn't necessary to go to college to get that skill—you can pick it up on your own. It can be anything—think about your hobbies, or summer jobs, or businesses you like to patronize. Anything that provides consumers with sustenance or pleasure is fair game. Do you like old houses? Get a real estate license. Or learn how to rebuild a staircase. Coupled with that skill, a philosophy degree will likely pay off for you. You'll be the lady who tells the carpenters what to do.

Art history can be an excellent major if coupled with a skill, for example web design. A person expert in the technology of social media (see Chapter 2) who also has an art history degree (and who is good at her job) will excel. English majors have a slight advantage in that good writing is itself a marketable skill, but failing that, any skill that you are good at will do. Without the skill, then, art history equals philosophy equals almost any liberal arts degree which, while it may not be worthless, does not lead easily to employment.

You need to decide what consumer product is going to pay your salary, where you are going to fit into the supply chain, and what skill you need to make that work. The skill will get you on to the career ladder, and the liberal arts degree will move you into a leadership role—assuming you are good at your job.

Don't Major in Fads

The third rule is also a reality check. Study subjects that are out of fashion.

In 2000, the TV show CSI premiered. Chemistry departments across the country were suddenly flooded with people who wanted to study forensic science. Now, forensic science is a real career, and there is nothing intrinsically wrong with it. But states and municipalities were not expanding their crime labs just because of some TV show. So the number of jobs in the discipline remained approximately the same, while the number of prospective candidates increased dramatically. You can guess what happened—salaries went down, and lots of new graduates were disappointed.

You have to be good in order to get a job, but when something becomes popular, such as forensic science, then you have to be even better. The odds are stacked against you.

Don't major in fads.

Computer gaming is a fad. There is a huge interest from high school boys, but no corresponding increase in the number of jobs. Likewise, any major with the word *environment* in it is probably a bad choice. Again, these disciplines have value, but the number of jobs is not increasing in any proportion close to the number of students. Stay away unless you're extremely good.

We're real nervous about nursing school. Nursing is a good major for the New Normal—it will not likely be automated. But there are so many people studying nursing right now that there looks to be a big glut on the horizon. The number of jobs just can't be increasing that quickly. Similar arguments hold for physical therapists, physician's assistants, or for that matter, physicians. The whole medical field looks to us as over-subscribed.

Case Study: Agriculture

A few years ago Dan had a student who enjoyed gardening and agriculture as a hobby. Along with a partner, he procured a few sunny acres of farmland on which they grew tomatoes and chili peppers. These they turned into a hot sauce that (as Dan can attest) is delicious. This got sold at farmer's markets, but their goal was to market it to restaurants.

To sell a food product at scale requires meeting Food & Drug Administration (FDA) guidelines. These affect everything from the product itself, to packaging, labeling and advertising.

While his business (as far as we know), never took off, the student became very familiar with these regulations.

All of this constitutes a very practical skill set in an incredibly valuable consumer market. Growing, cooking, packaging and selling a food product is not something one learns in school. Coupled with a bachelors degree in chemistry, this fellow is fantastically marketable to any number of companies anywhere along the food supply chain — food processors, bakeries, agricultural enterprises (such as a winery), restaurant chains, supermarket chains, and more besides. Just knowing something about the FDA puts him light years ahead of other biology or chemistry majors. He could have written his own ticket.

Did he do that? Unfortunately, not. Instead he chose to go to graduate school in chemistry so he could become a college professor. In our view, this is completely unrealistic — like he's never heard of the New Normal. Fortunately, his opportunities will likely still be there after he finishes grad school, so all he's doing is wasting time and money.

A second example is a young woman (whom we've never met) who is graduating with degrees in agriculture from Vermont Technical College. She tells her story in a podcast.[18] She was interested in any number of liberal arts subjects: she considered a law career, or majoring in psychology. Instead, she really enjoyed her summer job working on a farm. So instead of majoring in a liberal arts discipline, she majored in her summer job. This works, because just from the three-minute clip you can tell that she is very good at what she does. She hits all three of the points we listed above.

As she doesn't have a liberal arts background, she will have to work harder at the leadership skills necessary to advance in her profession. She'll have to engage some academic subjects on her own, such as literature, philosophy or art. Without the leadership skills, she'll just be a hired hand, albeit a very good one. Again, from her podcast, we have little doubt that she'll succeed, but this is backwards from the way most students do it.

We predict that she'll be spending many a Vermont winter evening reading books.

Study Questions:

1. We think biology is not a good college major right now. Does that mean nobody should major in biology? Why or why not?

2. Is the career you're thinking about a fad? What evidence do you have either way?

3. If you can, go talk to some college seniors who are near graduation. Choose those who are majoring in a field you're interested in. Find out what their employment prospects are. Ask if they have or will have an internship. Ask about their GPA. Try to get some sense about how good you have to be in order to be employed in that field.

4. What hobbies or experiences do you have that might constitute a marketable skill? What could you do to enhance that skill, and how can you include it on your resume?

SHOULD YOU GO TO COLLEGE?

Gourmet food and fine wine are good things. Most of us enjoy the occasional evening with family and friends at that special restaurant. If it can't happen often, it's a rare treat. If you go out every week, it's still enjoyable, though no longer a special event.

But if you go out every day for both lunch and dinner, then you're overdoing it. Too much good food and fine wine makes one fat and drunk.

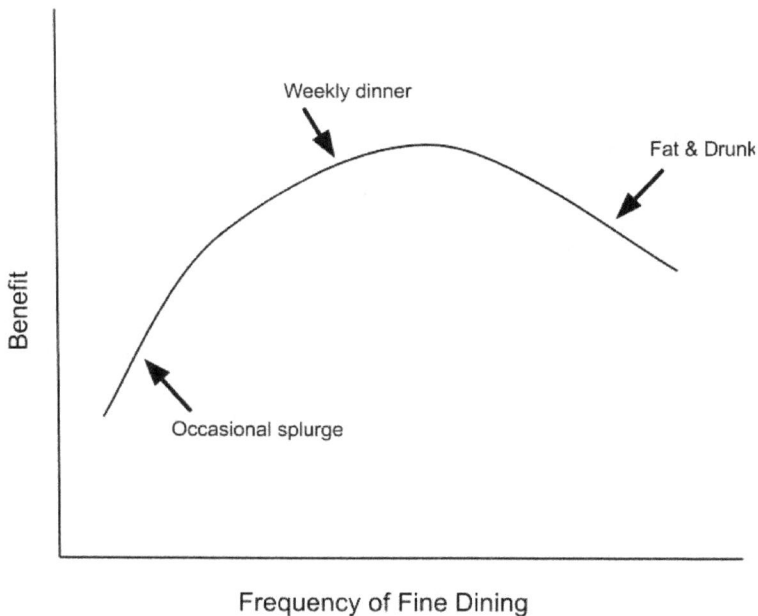

Figure 3: Cartoon diagram of fine dining experience

When infrequent, it's an evening you'll remember for a long time. Each meal is a special event; the marginal benefit is huge. As it becomes more common, it's still fun, but not as much. Meals, still enjoyable, become routine. That's shown in Figure 3. The hill levels off as you get closer to the top. The marginal benefit has shrunk—an example of the law of diminishing returns. It's still positive — you're climbing the hill — but not very positive. And as one gets fat and drunk, fine dining becomes counterproductive. The marginal benefit has gone negative. Now you're going downhill.

This is just an economist's fancy way of saying *too much of a good thing*, or repeating Aristotle's famous adage *all things in moderation*.

So everybody, including us, believes that a college education is a good thing—just like fine food. But just like food, one can get too much of it. We think that Americans spend too much money and time on college. We're at the *fat & drunk* stage. However good college may be in principle, we're overdoing it.

We base our opinion in part on the following data:

- It takes more time than ever to graduate. A bachelor's degree is supposed to be completed in four years. But these days it takes most students five or six years to complete that degree. Today, colleges measure their success by the six-year graduation rate.

- Approximately 40% of students who start college never graduate. As we detail below, these people would be better off if they'd never gone to college.

- Since 2007, increasing numbers of college graduates are not getting jobs for which a college degree is necessary. That leads to pizza deliverers with biology degrees.

- Student loans now total more than a trillion dollars— the situation has become a national scandal. Student loans are not dischargeable in bankruptcy, and they increasingly prevent young people from getting married, buying houses, or saving for retirement.

- The college curriculum is increasingly disconnected from reality. The modern college was designed in the 1950s and 1960s, and doesn't make much sense in the New Normal.

- Our anecdotal opinion is that a fair number of students in our classes are not doing well, and are not enjoying the experience. They're in college because somebody told them they had to do that—sort of like eating spinach.

Apparently, young people are beginning to catch on. The Department of Education reports that the college enrollment rate is declining. In 2011, 42.3% of recent high school grads entered a four-year college. In 2012 the number was 37.5%, or nearly a 5% decline. That's only for one year, but we hope it's the start of a trend.

So should you go to college?

Is College a Good Choice?

Actually, that question is pretty easy to answer.

- If you are good at school and you enjoy it, then by all means you should go to college. You need to make sure you follow the advice in the last chapter so you can get a job after you graduate—but it is very likely that college will pay off for you.

- If you are not good at school, or if you don't enjoy it, then you should *Drop Out Now* (or better yet, not go to college in the first place). Later in this book, we'll describe how you can build a career without going to college.

These rules apply whether you're attending a community college or a four-year school. One caveat: many people go to college for reasons that have little to do with a career. Perhaps you want to find a spouse, or play sports, or you enjoy the social life. Maybe you like school, just as some people enjoy going to movies. Those are all good reasons for going to college, but are beyond the scope of this book. Proceed at your own risk.

The worst thing you can do is go to college and then not graduate. The economist Bryan Caplan[19] cites some numbers that illustrate.

- If you graduate from a four-year college, you will earn on average 83% more than a high school graduate in a given year.
- If you have some college but don't graduate (more or less regardless if you attended for one year or three and a half years), you will earn on average about 10% more than a high school graduate.

This is called the *sheepskin effect*. It means that you really only benefit financially from college if you graduate. Just attending college is not enough—it won't help you much on the job market. (The sheepskin effect also applies to community college students, to a much lesser degree.)

So if you go to college, you need to be pretty darn certain that you're going to graduate. That's what leads to our advice above. If there is a significant risk that you're not going to graduate (and 40% of you won't), then you should cut your losses now. Don't waste any more of your time. Don't waste any more of your money. Don't take out any more student loans. *Drop Out Now*.

Dan recently counseled a biology major. She was in her fifth year of college, but had not yet passed general chemistry (this was her third try). Dan advised her to *Drop Out Now*—advice she happily accepted (she was just waiting for somebody to give her permission). So this young lady spent five years in school, and who knows how much money or how much she owes in loans, and has essentially nothing to show for it. There's a word for people like her: *screwed*.

Don't be like her. If you're not good at school, or if you don't enjoy it, then you will probably not finish. *Drop Out Now.*

Why Do Employers Like College Grads?

There are two principal reasons why employers prefer college graduates.

First, presumably they know something. Learning useful stuff in college is an investment in *human capital*. That should make you a more valuable employee, better able to create consumer benefit. Doctors, for example, have a big investment in human capital that makes it possible for them to do their jobs.

Second, graduating from college signals to employers that you have certain personality traits or skills that are likely to make you a good employee. This is called the *signaling effect*. The signaling effect is what accounts for the dramatic difference in outcomes between graduates and people who never finished.

What personality traits do you signal by graduating from college?

- Intelligence. People who graduate are generally smarter than people who don't graduate. But it isn't necessary to spend four years in college to demonstrate that you have a high IQ. An interviewer can probably establish your IQ in fifteen minutes. So the contribution of IQ to the sheepskin effect is probably small.

- Diligence. To graduate from college, you have to get the work done. If you can't get the work done, then it doesn't matter how smart you are. A lot of students (and parents) excuse themselves by saying, "He's really smart, but he doesn't always work very hard." But employers are looking for people who can get the work done, and graduating from college demonstrates that.

- Tolerance for boredom. A lot of college is taking boring classes and passing them with good grades. That (truth be told) is the principal reason for general education programs. Because not only is college like that, but work life is also like that. Employers don't want to hire you if you can't do boring.

- Dan had a student in a gen ed class who simply hated chemistry. With great self-discipline she came to class every day and did all the assignments. She will be golden to employers because she's proven she can power her way through a boring class. (She'll also never look at any *chemistry* again.)

- Follow directions. College is a big bureaucracy where a major part of success is just following directions. You need to take the right classes for graduation. You need to show up at the right place at the right time. You need to hand in assignments just the way the professor wants them, written this way and not that way. Yeah—they all brag about creativity and stuff, but that's not what college is really about. It's about following directions, because that's what employers want. Employers want you to work for them, not to go off and do your own thing. A college degree is an excellent signal.

- Conformity. Employers don't want to hire somebody who is going to rock the boat. You need to get along with your fellow workers and (especially) with the customers. Colleges enforce this through a smiley-faced political correctness. This is an imaginary world where everybody always gets along, nobody says anything impolite or offensive, there is no violence (or even discussion of violence), no sexual tension, and never a contrary word. Conservatives blame radical, leftist professors for this sorry state of affairs, but they're wrong. Politically correct is precisely how employers want you to treat their customers and fellow employees. To find a job, you need to put on that smiley-face and leave everything else at home. College is a great training ground, and the degree is an excellent signal that you can do it.

So if you drop out of college, it means you probably failed on one or more of these counts. Perhaps you're lazy, or you lack self-discipline, or you can't follow directions, or you can't keep the smiley face on firmly enough to get along with the faculty. Maybe you have reasons, or maybe there's a story, or whatever. But for the employer, there's always another resume to look at from somebody who doesn't come with baggage—somebody who graduated from college. The sheepskin effect rules.

This isn't good for society. Society needs nonconformists who chart their own way and don't follow directions. Society needs people like Steve Jobs (founder of Apple Computer) who survived college only for one year. Steve Jobs was a great entrepreneur, but he was a lousy employee—as his college career probably predicted.

Still, unless you're a genius like Steve Jobs, or determined enough to make it as an entrepreneur, or crazy enough to become a starving artist, the surest route to a good career is to graduate from college. You should do that if you can. If you can't (for whatever reason), you're going to have to put a signal together in some other way. We'll get to that later in this book.

Graduating from college doesn't mean you have to be a brown-nosing rule-follower for the rest of your life. While college graduates have a proven ability to follow the rules, they can also judge when and how to break them. College gives you the power to choose which rules to break.

Realistic Expectations

The above paints a pretty unflattering picture of college life. How different this is from the way colleges advertise themselves: *Maximize your potential; Show off your creativity; Demonstrate leadership; Sprout wings.* Some of that is just advertising hype, but not all of it. After all, professors don't try to be boring. And not all general education classes are tedious—some of them can be really interesting. (In defense of the faculty, boring exists mostly in the mind of the student.) A precious few general education classes will change your life—you'll discover a future career in something you'd never thought of before.

The sheepskin effect isn't what colleges want to be about. They really do aspire to be what they advertise. The sheepskin effect arises from what employers want in an employee. That disconnect between what colleges advertise and what employers want leads to graduates with hopelessly unrealistic expectations.

College students frequently imagine that they will graduate to thrilling, important jobs. This doesn't mean they'll move right into the corner office, but it does mean they will use the fascinating knowledge they have acquired. But that is very rarely the case.

College prepares you for an entry-level job, which at best will be the first rung on a career ladder. Entry-level jobs all have one, overriding characteristic—they're *boring*.

Law students aspire to get jobs with Big Law firms. These pay huge salaries to the best graduates. They get the best graduates because of the career track they (used to) promise. But the jobs pay well because nobody would do them except for the money—they are intensely tedious and meaningless. We mentioned the story[20] from the woman who lost her $230K job at Big Law during the recession, and now works as a small-town lawyer for $40K.

"There's probably a bankruptcy in our future. I don't think there's a way out of it," Helen told me. "In ten years, hopefully we'll be financially recovered, we can buy a house, have a credit card again." Before we hung up, I pointed out that the legal market had improved since 2010. Why not look for another fancy job in Chicago? "There's no way I would go back to Big Law," she said. "I'm doing a lot of criminal law now. I love it. It's originally what I'd intended to do when I went to law school."

The fun and meaningful jobs pay little and offer no career track. Indeed, the very best jobs are avocations—hobbies—things you do for free. High-paying, entry-level jobs are typically unremittingly tedious and meaningless.

Signaling

We have taken a look at the discipline we know best (chemistry), and asked *What part of the chemistry curriculum represents real education (i.e., human capital investment), and what part is mostly just signaling?* Put another way, what classes would you have to take to be prepared for an entry-level, professional job in a chemistry laboratory? Here is what we came up with:

- General Chemistry (2 classes, plus labs)
- Organic Chemistry (2 classes, plus labs)
- Analytical Chemistry (1 class, plus lab)
- Perhaps Biochemistry or Instrumental Analysis (or both, plus labs)
- Pre-calculus
- Physics (1 class, plus lab)
- English Composition

That's eight to ten classes, which, because they have to be taken in order, will require two years. This is not a community college curriculum—we're assuming the rigor and facilities typically found at a selective, four-year school. If human capital were all that counted, we think you could leverage this into professional employment as a chemist (if you were good enough).

Instead, beyond human capital development, students have to show the signal. That means, in addition to the above, the following is typically required for a bachelor's degree in chemistry:

- Four or five more chemistry classes, including some labs.
- Roughly ten additional general education classes.
- A year of calculus, along with a class in differential equations.
- An additional physics class.
- A research or capstone class.
- Additional classes to meet the required number of total credit hours.

While some of these classes may be useful, none of them are necessary for the entry level positions you qualify for right after graduation. They could all be taken later as needed, either on the job, as online classes, by self-study, or if laboratory facilities are necessary, on a campus.

The only reason these classes are required is because of the signal they provide to employers. That's great for employers— they get a vetting service that's completely free for them. It's pretty sweet for colleges, too—the extra revenue is wonderful. But students are getting ripped off.

There is a special kind of signaling that's even more restrictive—it's called *credentialing*. This is when the government requires you to get a license before you can engage in certain occupations. If you want to become a doctor or a lawyer, for example, you have to go to medical school or law school in order to get the license. Lots and lots of jobs require licenses these days: nurses, teachers, accountants, beauticians, real estate agents, interior decorators, financial advisors, electricians, etc., etc. Some people estimate that as many as a third of all occupations are now licensed.

While for many jobs you can conceivably signal your ability without a college degree, that is not possible when a license is required. There is no work-around. If you want to be a lawyer, you have to go to law school. Abraham Lincoln couldn't be a lawyer today.

College and The New Normal

So far, most of what we've said are timeless truths—as true in 1980 as they are today. But some things have changed because of the New Normal, and that's where we now turn.

The first change is, fewer students are going to college. The major reason for that is simple demographics—there are fewer high school students graduating today than before. But also, as we've already mentioned, a smaller percentage of them are going to college. This is at least partly because of the phenomenal rise in tuition costs—up an average 7.5% every year since 1978. That's compared with the average 3.8% inflation rate. College costs have grown faster than either home prices or medical care.

That's through 2011. Since then, tuition has begun to go down, as the law of supply and demand suggests it should.

A second change is technological disruption. While we doubt that online education will ever completely displace the in-person sort, it will certainly take over many functions. Grading chemistry homework, for example, is now mostly computerized. Math classes are arguably better taught online than in a classroom. Online has the advantage of being much cheaper. The result is that a large number of professors will be unemployed, and those still working will have different job descriptions than they do today. How that all works out, or how long it takes for big changes to happen, we have no idea. But we think that online competition is already putting downward pressure on tuition.

More important for you is that online opportunities make it possible to continue your education beyond your college years. When Dan was young, his parents told him, "You have one chance at college. You need to do that while you're young." That's not true anymore. Today, you can take college courses anywhere and any time. Indeed, we think that general education classes may be best taken online by older students already in the workforce. That's when you're mature enough to understand the value of what you're learning. Lifelong learning becomes not just a slogan, but a real possibility.

Online education makes it easier to *Drop Out Now*, if that's what you decide to do. You'll get a second chance at college later at a significantly lower price.

The third change is that in the past, a college degree pretty much entitled you to a middle class income. That is no longer true in the New Normal. Today, not only do you need the degree, but you also need to be *good enough* to get the job. How good you have to be depends on how many jobs there are, and how many people are majoring in your field. We discussed this in the last chapter.

The economist Tyler Cowen wrote a book titled *Average Is Over*,[21] where he argues that below-average employees will gradually lose their jobs. They'll be the first ones replaced by machines. The bottom line is, if you're a below average college student, you need to either *Change Majors Now* or *Drop Out Now*. It's more important than ever to be really good at what you do.

The final change due to the New Normal is that a college education is probably less important today than it was in the past.

The reason is that fewer employers are willing to make a long-term investment in their employees. More people work under short-term, piecework arrangements than did before. When you're hired short-term just to do a specific job, the employer really doesn't care much about your personality traits. The signal effect becomes unimportant, and employers no longer ask about a college degree.

Google is an example of a company that is less interested in your college background than most companies. In a recent article,[22] "Google's head of people operations, Laszlo Bock, detailed what the company looks for. And increasingly, it's not about credentials." Google's employees are overwhelmingly young. Nobody knows what will happen to these people when they reach middle age, but our anecdotal evidence suggests that Google is not planning on long-term relationships with its employees. The signal doesn't matter.

Keeping It Real

If you go to college (and also if you don't), it is very important to keep your eyes wide open. You can't believe all the advertising hype you'll get from various sources.

- Employers will tell you there is a desperate shortage of certain skills, e.g., social media experts. Don't believe it. While there may be a very few niche exceptions (petroleum engineers—and do you really want to put all your eggs in that basket?), wages across the economy are flat. There is no evidence of any widespread skills shortage. You will have to struggle for a job no matter what you major in, and you will have to be good at what you do.

- Remember that a college degree will at best qualify you for an entry-level job. The skills you develop through your senior research project will probably not be required.

- Colleges will try to sell you on fun and fulfilling things, like *research opportunities* or *study abroad*. These extras may not improve your job prospects much unless directly related to some practical skill, such as foreign language fluency. Their primary effect is to increase your costs, lengthen your time to degree, and generate revenue for the college. If you enjoy these activities, fine, but be aware that they're probably not advancing your career.

- *Nobody can predict the future, but you know more about your future than anybody else.* Keep that in mind when talking to the faculty. The faculty will gently but persistently encourage you to follow in their footsteps. Never mind that they came of age in a different time and under different circumstances. Their advice is usually well-intentioned, but be very careful before you follow it. They will often, for example, encourage you to go to graduate school. That's because they went to grad school and were successful at it. Back in the day that was a good option. Today, not so much.

- Indeed, never go to graduate school if you can avoid it. With a bachelor's degree, you already have way more formal schooling than you need. There is no additional signaling benefit from grad school. Indeed, we think grad school is mostly for people who weren't good enough to get jobs when they first graduated.

- In some cases, you may have no choice. If you need a credential, then you have to go to grad school, for example if you want to be a doctor or a lawyer. Otherwise, if you're good at your profession, then grad school isn't necessary, and if you're not good, then grad school won't help. It marks you as a 'loser.'

- Don't pay more for college than you need to. Public schools are often cheaper than private schools, and are therefore usually a better deal. Don't let yourself be flattered by scholarships—all private colleges will do that.

Financial aid is offered not to benefit you, but rather to maximize revenue for the college. After all, they'd much rather discount the price from $20K to $15K instead of having you go spend your money elsewhere. Compare prices after all financial aid is accounted for.

- Avoid student loans if at all possible. Don't let anybody tell you that they're a form of financial aid. They are not—instead they are a very dangerous trap. We'll have more to say about that in the next chapter. A good rule of thumb is to never take out student loans for your freshman year. Then if you decide to *Drop Out Now* you're not totally screwed over. Don't go to a college you can't afford.

- Colleges are not all the same. Oddly enough, it's the students who determine how good a college is. That's because teachers teach to the students they've got rather than to some hypothetical standard. The better the students, the higher the academic rigor. The best quick way to judge a school is to look at the average SAT scores of enrolled freshmen. You want to choose schools where you are slightly above average, but not far above average.

Case Study: Government Jobs

One of the ways in which colleges have not kept up with the times is that too many majors prepare one for government employment. This may have worked in the 1970s and 1980s, but it doesn't work in the New Normal.

Almost all education majors expect to work for the government. People who major in sociology (especially criminology) can only work for the state. Many health care workers are employed by the state, as are most college professors. Geographers and civil engineering majors mostly plan on working for the government.

So what's wrong with that?

On the one hand, nothing. Society will always need civil engineers, police officers, and welfare case workers, not to mention teachers. Historically, these jobs have paid relatively well. Indeed, there is now some resentment against government workers as being overpaid, especially in terms of benefits such as pensions and health care. On average[23] (as of 2010) 15.3% of American workers are employed by government at all levels, ranging from 27% in Alaska to 11.9% in Pennsylvania.

In the New Normal there are not as many government jobs as there used to be, and those jobs are increasingly unattractive. That message hasn't gotten through to colleges yet, who continue to prepare students for unrealistic job opportunities. We've already mentioned forensic science—a category where student interest is completely out of whack with available jobs. Students who aspire to jobs in environmental protection or astrophysics are similarly likely to be disappointed.

Two big government agencies are shedding jobs. Active duty military personnel decreased from over 2 million in 1990 to just under 1.4 million today. Similarly, the postal service has shrunk from 760,000 employees in 1987 to 490,000 today. Especially for postal employees, future prospects are grim.[24]

A big reason for the decline in these agencies is technological disruption. E-mail and other electronic communications have reduced first class mail volume by half. Even so-called *junk mail* has been declining in volume, though not as dramatically, displaced by the Internet. Military personnel are increasingly replaced by robots, such as drone aircraft.

Many government services are being automated. Dan, for example, recently renewed his driver's license over the web. Welfare checks have been replaced by EBT cards, with similar arrangements made for social security payments. While government responds more slowly to cost-saving technology than private business, it does respond. Large numbers of government bureaucrats are slowly losing their jobs. Similar sorts of disruption is coming to schools and universities soon.

Sometimes, technology only indirectly threatens jobs. Over the last forty years, there have been major improvements in building codes, along with serious efforts to increase the use of smoke detectors, etc. The result is that the number of major fires is at an all-time low. We simply don't need as many firefighters as we have.[25] For sentimental reasons, they all remain employed (nobody wants to lay off the heroes), but perhaps not for very long.

Besides technology, there are two other reasons why government employment will likely decline. The first is the stagnant or even declining population. From 2000 to 2010 the US population increased by only 10%, the smallest fraction in our history. Population growth looks set to decline more in the coming decade, or even go into reverse. That means fewer schools, fewer new roads, fewer prisons, and fewer government employees. Government is definitely not a growth industry.

The second reason is even more serious. Governments across the country (and for that matter, around the world) are deeply in debt. Journalist Kevin Williamson[26] estimates that US governments at all levels are in hock for $300 *trillion*. That's more money than exists in the entire universe! That figure includes future social security, pension, and medical obligations, along with the usual expenses of government.

It will never all get paid. We've already seen the tip of the iceberg with the bankruptcy of Detroit, along with some cities in California. Puerto Rico and Illinois are bankrupt in every way except in name. California and New Jersey are not far behind. Many, many cities, counties, and school districts will fail financially, especially those where the population is declining.

So our advice is to just stay out of it. Avoid working for the government if you can. On the other hand, if that's what you really want to do, count on stiff competition for those jobs. You'll have to be really, really good.

Study Questions:

1. Look at the list of majors at the college you're thinking of attending. Which major do you think you would be best at?

2. What hobby or part-time job do you have that can lead to consumer benefit? How can you develop that into something you can put on your resume? What connection can you make between that and the major you are good at?

3. Suppose you've attended college for a semester. You want to study medicine, but you've gotten a C in your chemistry class. What should you consider doing?

4. Suppose you've attended college for a semester. What would have to happen before you *Drop Out Now*?

5. Are there any government jobs that, despite our advice, you really want to have? What's your best bet to making that a reality? How can you protect yourself in case your dreams don't come true?

6. Knowing what you now know about how college generates a signal, how will that change your attitude toward education?

CAPITAL

There aren't very many books about careers that have a chapter entitled *Capital*. But choosing a career is an *investment decision*, and understanding some of the language of business is useful.

Suppose your parents promised you $40,000 for tuition, but you played a little trick on them. Instead of going to college, you put the money into the stock market. You invested it in a Standard & Poor's (S&P) index fund, which means you'd own a bit of the 500 large companies that dominate the US economy. And then you forgot about it—the money sits there collecting dividends (a share of the profits) and capital gains (an increase in the value of the company).

We can't predict the future, but if Dan or Tom had done that back in 1966 (assume we were 18 years old then, and that a year of college back then only cost $5,500), then 47 years later in 2013 when we finally remembered that we'd stashed away that money, it would be worth $487,000.[27]

You could retire on that if you had to! Even if you never saved another penny over the rest of your career.

This is an example of the *law of compound interest*. This says that because of interest, a little bit of money is added to your savings every month, but the amount added next month is always greater than the amount added this month. Accordingly, you end up with a balance that grows *exponentially*, as this chart indicates. The longer you wait, the more money you will have.

The dollar you save today is worth more than any dollar you will save later in life. If you start saving at age 18 you are compounding your money for 47 years (if you retire at age 65). On the other hand, waiting until age 30 to stash the $5,500 results in a nest egg only worth $309,000. Starting at age 50 only nets $14,000.

So you need to start saving today. Your parents may not be able to spot you $5,500 (or $40,000 in today's dollars), but if you can beg $1,000, or even $500 out of them, that's probably enough to get you into a mutual fund. And then you need to add to it every month, even if it's only a little bit. Saving $50 a month for the rest of your career beginning at age 20 at 5% annual interest will net you $102,000 by the time you retire.

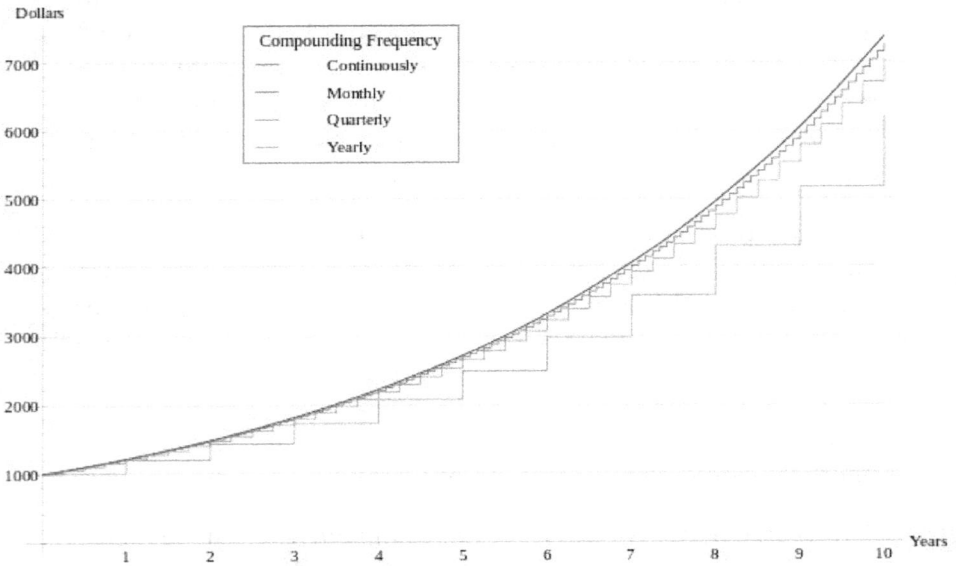

Figure 4: The effect of compound interest.[28]
The staircase illustrates the description in the text. Note that each step is bigger than the previous one.

Inflation & Deflation

Your parents probably grew up during the 1970s, and they probably remember high inflation. Inflation is a measure of how much prices rise on average in a given year. It hit 11.0% in 1974, and 13.5% in 1980, as shown in Figure 5.

Inflation Rate, 1970-2014

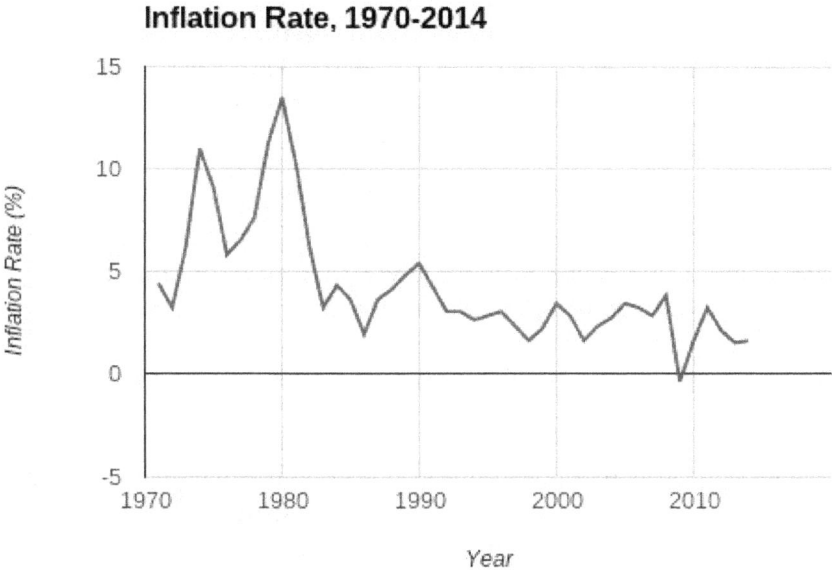

Figure 5: Inflation Rate from 1970 to 2014.[29]

Your parents are used to correcting everything for inflation. We did that in our example above. We took the money our parents gave us for tuition at a public college, worth approximately $40,000 today, and estimated what that would have cost in 1966. That's where the $5,500 came from, and this is how we corrected our calculation for inflation. That money was then invested in the S&P index fund, yielding an average of 9.72% annually (see endnote 27). Compounded over 47 years, we got $487,000.

There's another way we could've corrected for inflation. Instead of starting with $5,500 in 1966 dollars, we could have saved the tuition in 2013 dollars, namely $40,000. But then all of our returns have to be adjusted for inflation. That means instead of a 9.72% rate, when adjusted for inflation we only get 5.33% average yield. That rate, compounded for 47 years, results in a fund worth $483,000, or just about the same, as you would expect.

The raw interest rate, unadjusted for inflation (in our example, 9.72%) is called the *nominal rate of return*. That's the money you actually get (and eventually pay taxes on), but it ignores the fact that each dollar buys less and less.

When you adjust for inflation, the interest rate is called the *real rate of return* (in our example, 5.33%). That number represents the actual spending power of your money. Or put another way, it's a measure of how comfortable your retirement will be. The problem is that inflation can only be approximately measured, and therefore real rates of return are just estimates.

While nominal rates of return have fluctuated with inflation, real rates of return have remained much more constant. From 1871 to 1966 the real rate of return is estimated at 7.41%, or higher than the 5.33% since 1966. (The further back in history you go, the less accurate the measure of inflation, so take these numbers with a grain of salt. How much did a cell phone cost in 1871?)

Most people (including us) assume that real rates will hover around 5%. Real rates go down when inflation gets really high, as in the 1970s. Those were bad years for the stock market. But in general, assuming a 5% real return on a long-term investment in a diversified stock portfolio is a reasonable, conservative estimate.

Very recently, a young French economist, Thomas Piketty,[30] has made a splash by predicting that real rates of return will be rising substantially over the next several decades. We have no idea if that's true, but it's all the more reason to start saving now.

The opposite of inflation is *deflation*. That means that prices go down over time. The last era of sustained deflation was during the Great Depression, when prices declined every year from 1927 to 1933. Deflation hit -10% in both 1932 and 1933. As we discussed in Chapter 3, we believe a reason for this was the automation of agriculture, sharply lowering prices for foodstuffs.

We won't claim to predict the future, but we think we may be entering another extended period of deflation. Our current round of automation will reduce costs for manufactured goods across the board, driving down prices. In addition, the population of both our country and the globe will not grow very much, and perhaps even start to decline. This will put downward pressure on the prices of housing and food.

Of course there are other factors that determine the inflation rate. In particular, government has some control over the money supply. But we suggest that government doesn't have anywhere near as much control over inflation as they think they do. (And what control they do have requires that they completely destroy the economy first.) Deflation is becoming a perennial problem in the Eurozone and in Japan, where populations are declining.

So your parents' presumption of inflation is unwarranted. There is at least a good chance that deflation will be the trend for much of your working life. Even without actual deflation, inflation looks to stay low, at 2% or below, for the foreseeable future. You need to think about both contingencies in planning your future. Let's consider the consequences of inflation and deflation separately.

Inflation

- If you borrow money, because of inflation the value of the amount you borrow goes down. This effectively lowers your interest rate. Thus, borrowing is relatively cheap.

- If you plan for inflation, then protecting yourself against rising interest rates is important. The 30-year, fixed-rate mortgage is a good way to do that. That charges you a higher interest rate now as an insurance premium against higher inflation in the future.

- Your salary will go up to account for inflation. That means debts you incurred when you were younger become relatively cheaper. In inflationary times, student loans are much safer because you'll be paying them back with cheaper dollars.

- Inflation is good for borrowers and spendthrifts. It is bad for creditors and savers. Cash will never be worth more than it is today, so you should probably spend it now. We note that very high inflation, such as occurred in the 1970s, is bad for everybody.

- In the 1970s, we were very worried about people living on fixed incomes, i.e., retirees who got a pension that didn't adjust for inflation. The value of that pension continuously decreased because of inflation.

- Inflation is good for governments. Governments are deep in debt, and are counting on inflation to eat away at that obligation. That's why governments around the world are struggling (not very successfully) to try to keep inflation above 2%.

Deflation

- If you borrow money, the amount you owe goes up in real terms. That's because the dollar you pay today is worth more than the dollar you borrowed yesterday. Borrowing is expensive.

- If you plan for deflation, then paying a premium to lock in interest rates is a waste of money. Instead of a 30-year, fixed-rate mortgage, you should take out an adjustable rate mortgage (ARM) with the lowest possible interest rate.

- In a deflation world, your salary will never go up, and might even go down. Employees at Dan's school haven't gotten a raise in at least five years. Your standard of living might go up because prices will get cheaper, but any debt you owe becomes relatively more expensive.

- Deflation is good for savers and creditors. You will be paid back in dollars that are worth more than what you saved/lent before. You should save every penny you can. We note that extreme deflation, such as in the 1930s, is bad for everybody.

- Today we're not especially worried about people on fixed incomes. On the contrary, we're more worried about people on "unfixed" incomes, e.g., social security recipients. Social security payments have declined because the cost-of-living adjustment is negative, i.e., deflation.

- Deflation is terrible for governments. They are deeply in debt and will have to pay it back in deflated dollars. Because everybody will be earning less money (in nominal terms) they won't be able to raise the tax revenue they could previously.

Why Should You Worry About Retirement?

When you're 18 years old, retirement seems impossibly far away. It is simply not human nature to plan that far into the future. That's why we have a social security system that obligates people to save for retirement.

Still, the odds very strongly favor that you will retire—it's much more likely than graduating from college. Of 100,000 men born 65 years ago, 80,000 of them are still alive and are retiring today. For women, the number is 88,000. Further, those men will on average live another 17 years, and the women 20 years. Life expectancy for somebody who is 18 years old today is 77 for men and 81 for women. That assumes no improvement in medical care.[31]

Economic trends will likely benefit savers more than spenders, even if there is no deflation. The best investment is probably in the stock market, but you can save money in your house as well. Even if you don't retire (or decide to retire before age 65) having a good nest egg will help. At the very least, you can leave something for your children. *Save Money Now.*

Student Loans

The interest rate for the 2014-15 academic year for federal student loans[32] is 4.66%, considerably higher than the rate for the previous year—3.86%. (Interest rates for the 2015-16 academic year remain at 4.66%.) Federal student loans come in two varieties—subsidized and unsubsidized—both of which carry the same interest rate.

A *subsidized student loan* is one where the government pays the interest on the loan for as long as you are in school at least half time. In addition, after you finish school, you can receive a *deferment*, during which time interest accrues on the loan, but you are not required to make payments. To receive a subsidized student loan, you need to demonstrate *financial need*. You apply for that by filling out the FAFSA application for federal financial aid. Your college determines the extent of your need, and thus how much you can borrow in subsidized student loans.

Because the interest is paid for by the government while you are in school, colleges often consider these loans to be financial aid. We think that's slightly dishonest, or at least not the whole truth. You are still required to pay off the entire amount that you borrowed, plus any interest that accrues after you leave school.

An *unsubsidized student loan* is one where there is no subsidy, and interest accrues from the day you take out the loan. However, you are not usually required to make payments on the loan while you are still in school—this is called a *forbearance period*. In addition, you may also receive a deferment for the six months after you finish school. Note that even though you are making no payments, the interest is accumulating on the loan. We say that the interest is being *capitalized*, i.e., added to the amount that you have borrowed. You will need to pay all of that back!

As there is no subsidy for unsubsidized loans, there is no way this can be considered financial aid. Indeed, you do not need to fill out a FAFSA to receive an unsubsidized loan. But colleges often advertise this as financial aid—a straight-out lie.

So let's do some math. We won't explain all the details of how we did the calculations, but we have tried to produce numbers as close as possible to what you would actually have to pay. Student loans are often repayable in 10 years after any forbearance or deferment, though that varies by individual circumstance. We'll use 10 years in our calculations.

> Case 1: $10,000 subsidized loan, borrowed in freshman year, no deferment, inflation assumed 0%.

So, you borrow $10,000 at the beginning of your freshman year. Because the loan is subsidized, upon graduation you still owe $10,000 four years later—the government has paid all the interest. After graduation, your payment will be $104.27 per month for ten years. You will pay a total of $12,512 over the course of the loan. This assumes there are no late fees or other penalties.

Case 2: $10,000 unsubsidized student loan, borrowed in freshman year with initial repayment after graduation, assuming 0% inflation.

You're still borrowing $10,000, but now the interest is being capitalized while you are still in school. Assuming you make no payments for four years, you will owe $12,048 upon graduation. Paying that off over ten years will cost you $125.62 every month. Over the course of the loan, you will pay $15,074, again assuming no late fees or penalties. This is about $2,500 more than the subsidized loan, which represents the value of the government subsidy.

Because we've assumed no inflation for the above examples, the real interest rate and the nominal interest rate are the same thing. But now let's factor in possible inflation or deflation. In Case 3 we'll assume a 2% inflation rate. That means that your salary goes up by an average of 2% per year during the course of the loan. And each dollar buys 2% less than what it bought before. So while the checks you will be writing every month will be exactly the same as in our previous examples, in reality you'll be getting a good deal.

Case 3: $10,000 unsubsidized student loan, as in Case 2, but assuming 2% inflation.

While the nominal rate for your loan remains 4.66%, the real rate is 2% less, since you'll be paying it back with less valuable dollars. Thus the real interest rate is 2.66%. Doing the calculation with that rate, you will owe $11,123 in real dollars at graduation, your monthly payment in real dollars will be $105.57 for ten years, and the total amount you'll pay will be only $12,668 over the course of the loan. That's less than $15,074.

Your checkbook won't know the difference. In nominal dollars you'll still be paying the $15,074. But in terms of your standard of living, i.e., as a proportion of your salary and other expenses, it will be as if your payments had gone down.

YOUR FUTURE JOB

In a world with a 5% real rate of return on capital, a 2.66% real interest rate isn't a bad deal. This is the bargain your parents got if they borrowed money in the 1980s or 1990s.

But what happens in a deflation world?

> Case 4: $10,000 unsubsidized student loan, as in Case 2, but assuming -1% deflation.

Given a nominal rate of 4.66%, with -1% deflation the real interest rate is now 5.66%. Working the numbers, you will owe $12,540 in real dollars upon graduation. Payments will come to $136.86 in real dollars per month, for a total bill of $16,423.

Again, your checkbook won't know the difference. You'll still be writing checks for $125.62 in nominal dollars. But meanwhile, every year, your salary is going down by an average of 1%, and prices for everything else are declining. This loan will eat up a bigger and bigger part of your budget.

In an inflation world—the one experienced by your parents and professors—student loans are not terrible. Your paycheck will generally keep up with inflation, which means the loan gets relatively cheaper and cheaper. Even a small increase in your salary because of extra schooling may well pay for itself.

But in a deflation or zero-inflation world—such as what we have now (more or less)—the shoe is on the other foot. You won't be getting any raises, and in the worst case your salary will be going down.

While it is true that college tuition has skyrocketed, and also that the interest rates on student loans has gone up significantly in the past few years, one of the main reasons student loans have become such a scandal is that deflation (or near enough) has raised the real interest rate impossibly high. Fewer people can pay them off any more.

If (like us) you think that deflation will continue or get worse over the next decade or two, then student loans are not a good option. They may be justified if you're a top student in engineering or computer science, and possibly also for medical school. But they are very risky.

If, on the other hand, you believe that inflation will return to what it was in previous decades, then student loans can be a relatively cheap way to borrow money.

There is another kind of student loan that your parents can take out on your behalf. It is called the Parent PLUS loan. These are all unsubsidized (that is, your parents start paying interest on day one), and usually don't come with any deferment (the bills are due immediately upon disbursement). The major difference is the interest rate—for PLUS loans for 2014-15 it is 7.21%!

In a deflation world of -1%, this results in a real interest rate of 8.2%. By comparison, home mortgage rates are around 3%, and you can buy a car on time paying about 5% interest. This rate is simply extortionate. Unless your child is a workaholic genius, there is almost no way this will ever pay for itself as an investment.

There is one more very important fact about all student loans— they are not dischargeable in bankruptcy. If you go bankrupt, a court determines how your assets get distributed to your creditors—who then have to take whatever they can get. You get to keep a little bit to live on, but all your remaining property is liquidated to pay what you owe. After that, your debts are wiped clean and you get to start over from zero. Technically, we say that debts are *discharged* in bankruptcy.

There are two kinds of debts that can't be discharged in bankruptcy—tax debt, and student loan debt. You will continue to owe those bills no matter what, until the day you die. They will garnish your social security checks to pay off your student loan debt. Student loan debt is even worse than what you owe the taxman. The latter is occasionally willing to negotiate and accept partial payment. That is almost never true of student loan debt. They are famous for never discounting anything.

Indeed, if you're late on payments they will add penalties, fees, and surcharges (not to mention interest) that will significantly add to your debt.

If you want to ever get married, or buy a house, or start a business, or even just get a credit card like normal people, defaulting on student loan debt is a very bad idea. Be aware of that risk before you take out student loans in the first place.

Investing in Yourself

Investment refers to money one puts aside in hopes of having more money in the future. You buy a stock, expecting that it will go up in price, and/or pay a nice dividend. Unfortunately, not all stocks behave that way. The restaurant discounter, Groupon, was worth over $26 per share in November, 2011, but is trading at $6.22 today. That was not a good investment.

The chance that an investment might not pay off is called the *risk*. A *high-risk* investment may deliver a large reward, e.g., double your money in a few months. But it can also crash to zero. In general, investors make risky investments expecting that they will earn a lot more than average. If the market on average yields about 5%, then a risky stock may need to pay back 10% in order to attract investors. That difference is called the *risk premium*.

For stocks, risk is measured by a number called *beta*. A diversified stock portfolio (which pays an average of 5%) is assigned a beta of 1. Riskier investments have beta values greater than 1. Relatively safe investments, on the other hand, have beta values less than 1. Groupon, for example, has beta equal 1.43, which is quite risky. The electric utility, Consolidated Edison, has beta equal to 0.17, and is very safe. (You can find the beta for any stock by searching for "*company name* stock beta." For example, we searched for "Groupon stock beta.")

If you want to make a killing on the market and get rich quick, you'll buy stocks like Groupon. Of course you can just as quickly lose all your money. If, on the other hand, you want to preserve your capital and are willing to live with a low rate of return, then Consolidated Edison is the stock for you.

Buying stocks is an example of investing in *financial capital*. You can invest in other things as well. For example, you can buy a house or rental property. That is known as *real estate*. Contrary to popular opinion, residential real estate has a very low rate of return—after inflation it is estimated to be only 0.7% over the long term. On the other hand, houses are very good places to live.

Another form of investment is *capital equipment*. If you want to open a restaurant, for example, you'll need to buy a stove, refrigerator, tables & chairs, etc. You will have to include an appropriate return on that investment when you set prices on your new menu.

Investing in your career is an example of *human capital*. Like all other forms of capital, it needs to generate a return in order to be worthwhile. The return may also include a *risk premium*, i.e., for some jobs you're more likely to be unemployed later in life than for others. As we discussed this in Chapter Two, acquiring very specialized skills will lead to a higher paying job now, but an increased risk of unemployment later as your skills become obsolete. These are jobs with a high risk premium. On the other hand, if you major in English or math, the risk premium is very low since those skills will always be in demand. Accordingly, the starting salaries are also much lower.

The difference in starting salaries between, say, an engineer and a social worker is in part that the risk premium for engineers is much higher. Another reason for the salary difference is that it is more difficult to become a good engineer than a good social worker, and hence good engineers are harder to find—their salaries are bid up.

It is possible to make a rough estimate on the return on invest-ment in education. This is what the people at payscale.com[33] attempt to do. They collect data on 1,312 colleges in the United States, and compare the return on investment with the cost of education. There are a whole bunch of different ways to do the calculation, but payscale.com's estimate of the annual return on investment (ROI) seems most useful for us.[34]

For example, the school with the greatest ROI is for students paying in-state tuition at Georgia Institute of Technology (Georgia Tech). Their return is 11.9% — a very healthy payback. Payscale.com puts the total cost for a bachelors degree at Geor-gia Tech at $92,000, including tuition, room and board, and an allowance that you are not working full time while going to school. By surveying alumni, they found that the average student earns $756,000 more than a high school grad over twenty years following graduation. From that they calculate the annual ROI, 11.9%. Note that Georgia Tech is mostly an engineering school, so graduates go on to high-paying jobs, which explains the high rate of return. Also note that only 79% of all students graduate — those that don't certainly receive a much lower return.

At the other extreme, the worst schools have a negative ROI, sometimes -10% or lower. Graduates from these schools earn less than a high school graduate over twenty years. From a financial standpoint there is no reason to attend these colleges. (Note that the payscale.com data is probably inaccurate for the specific schools at the bottom of the list. Do not take it too literally.)

Rather than thinking about payscale's estimated ROI of the school you want to attend, it is probably more useful to con-sider your own likely ROI. If you are good at your major and at what you do, then the investment will likely pay off for you. It's as if you were putting money into a good stock.

If, on the other hand, you have a mediocre GPA, or you don't enjoy your studies very much, then your likely ROI may not be very high. That's a clue to either *Drop Out Now*, or major in something that's easier for you.

It is interesting that the median[35] ROI is 5.0%—pretty much matching what you'd expect from the stock market. Thus, *on average*, investing in education is as valuable as putting your tuition dollars in a diversified stock fund, at least if payscale. com data is to be believed.

We don't totally believe payscale's results, even though they've done the best they could with the data available to them. They compare earnings of college grads with earnings of high school grads, and then correct for the time students spend in college (while the HS grads are working). The assumption is that the only difference between HS grads and college grads is that the latter graduated from college. But that's not true. As we showed in the last chapter, college grads have certain personality traits that will make them more successful whether or not they go to college. Hence we think that college has less of an effect on your future earnings than payscale.com implies. We do not know how much less.

We do think that investment in education is inherently more risky than investment in a diversified stock portfolio, despite the fact that the median ROI is the same in both cases. This is because of the word *diversified*. That means you buy lots of different stocks—some will go down and some will go up, but on average you'll get a 5% return. With education, on the other hand, you cannot diversify. You can only major in one (or maybe two) disciplines. You are then very much at the mercy of how the marketplace treats your acquired skill.

Looking at the payscale.com rankings, you will see that the elite schools come in near the top, especially if they offer engineering programs. These are the schools where the best, very smartest students attend, and it makes sense that they'd earn the most. This is not primarily because they went to college, but because *they are very good at what they do*. If you're very good at what you do, then your risk is pretty low, and you'll earn a high salary because good people are always in short supply. You should definitely go to college.

For weaker students the risk becomes much greater. Indeed, you can easily lose on your investment, just as you can invest in a bad stock. And this brings us back to the advice in the last chapter. If you are *good at school and you enjoy it*, then you should probably go to college. If, on the other hand, you are just average or below average, your ROI is likely not going to be very high. You'd be better off taking the tuition money and putting it in a diversified stock portfolio.

You need to take a hard-headed look at yourself and judge if you are good enough at your chosen career to warrant additional investment. If not, save the money and do something else.

The rest of this book is about other ways you can invest in yourself besides education. Among other things, we will suggest ways you can put a good signal together without paying for four years of college.

Case Study: Finance

"My people will talk to your people."

That's the cliché used to describe how the details of business deals are put together. After the principals have sketched out the big picture, it's up to the accountants, the lawyers, the IT folks, and maybe the engineers to figure out how it goes down in practice.

The phrase won't work in the New Normal. Instead, they'll say "my computer will talk to your computer."

The fact is that computers already hold most of the data. All human beings do is a few additional layers of processing and synthesis—steps that can be computerized as easily as anything else. In a word, the computers can increasingly implement the bosses' strategy by themselves.

Students who graduate from elite institutions often end up on Wall Street. An article[36] from *The Atlantic* describes the unhappy life of junior bankers—the long hours, the deadly tedious jobs, the lack of any meaningful purpose. Even the salaries—up to $140,000—strike us as pretty chintzy given the cost of living in New York.

The major reason these jobs pay so much is because they are horrible jobs—nobody would do them for less. The only other reason to take them is that they put you on a career track, supposedly worth millions down the line.

But just as with lawyers, that career track is now drying up. More and more banking and finance jobs can be done by computers, especially the boring ones.

When Dan and Tom were teenagers, the New York Stock Exchange (NYSE) operated on *open outcry*. If you went to your broker in Eugene, OR or Philadelphia, PA, or wherever, and wanted to sell 100 shares of AT&T (nicknamed *Ma Bell* in those days), the broker picked up the phone (or perhaps it moved by teletype) and called his office in New York. The clerk in New York wrote your request on a piece of paper, which was given to a *runner*. The runner was a human being tasked to take this piece of paper onto the trading floor. Trading was done in pits, with each traded stock (in your case, AT&T) assigned to one of the pits. The runner took your scrap of paper to the trader representing your brokerage at that pit.

That trader conducted an auction right there on the spot. Using shorthand code and hand signals, he'd cry out, "I'm selling 100 shares of AT&T. Is there a buyer at $30?" Other traders with buy orders made bids on your shares, and your trader accepted the highest bid. That many other auctions were happening in the same pit simultaneously created an illusion of total chaos.

Of course, all these people wanted to be paid: the stock broker, the clerk, the runner, the trader, along with all of their counterparts on the buyer's side of the deal. Trading stocks in the 1960s was very, very expensive, and essentially a preserve of the wealthy.

Today most of those folks are unemployed. The broker has been replaced by a webpage. The runner obviously isn't necessary anymore. Computers can negotiate the trades directly, without any human intervention. Accordingly, anybody can trade stocks today—a whole cottage industry of day traders sprang up in the aughts, before the 2007 crash. You can see it in the numbers. A typical day in 1968 resulted in about 4 million shares changing hands. Today often as many as a billion shares trade—a 250-fold increase.

So today, if you want to sell 100 shares of AT&T and Tom wants to buy 100 shares of AT&T, then quite literally, Tom's computer talks to your computer. This automation process has accelerated sharply over the past few years. Trading algorithms and high frequency trading are two examples where computers do all the work. Those elite-school college grads no longer have a very secure future in front of them.

But people will always be involved. The finance industry will never be completely automated. There are at least three ways people will stay in the loop.

First, the very phrase *my computer will talk to your computer* suggests that there is a "me" and a "you" responsible for the computer. If you don't want to sell your shares, then our computers have nothing to talk about. And ultimately, it's human beings who have money, who care about investing, and who buy and sell stocks, and who can go to jail if something goes horribly wrong. The intermediaries will get iced out, but the principals are necessarily still in the business. The human beings take the risks and keep the profits—not the computers.

Even this gets fudged. Trading algorithms are computer programs that implement a given trading strategy. A human being delegates the authority to the computer to make individual trades. So the 100 shares of AT&T that you want to sell may, indeed, be bought by a computer with no human involvement at all. But a human being is still responsible. It's the human who is legally responsible for paying you money for your shares, whatever the computer may have decided on his behalf.

Second, most of us are not very good at buying and selling shares. We simply don't have the tools or experience. So we rely on *financial advisors* to help us out. These people are usually salesmen for a financial services firm, such as Vanguard, or TIAA-CREF. They provide an essential service, and for that they receive a commission. While they need to be knowledgeable, it is essential that they be personable. They are salesmen and counselors first, and financial whizzes only secondarily.

Finally comes the question of trust. If Dan asked Tom to lend him $10,000, it just might work. We've known each other for thirty years, and Tom has probably learned to trust Dan. But if Dan's friend Andy (whom Tom has never met) asked for the same favor, the deal would never happen. There's not enough trust.

Any kind of banking depends on trust. One can partially computerize this—that's what credit scores and credit reports are for. And that works well for relatively small amounts such as car loans or home mortgages where there is some collateral. But for bigger amounts that are not collateralized—say, for example, the billions of dollars of overnight loans that banks make to each other—it has to rely on trust.

Felix Martin, in his wonderful little book *Money: The Unauthorized Biography*,[37] describes the origin of modern banking in the 17th Century. The village moneylender trusted his fellow villagers enough to lend them money. He, in turn, borrowed his capital from a big merchant in town, whom he knew personally. That merchant borrowed money from the big moneylender in the City, again on the basis of personal trust. And those big moneylenders—today we'd call them bankers—met once a year at a fair in Lyon to square accounts. During the year they borrowed money from each other on the basis of trust.

You can only trust a human being, and so banking will always depend on people. *Can I trust you?* is the question every banker has to ask. That's why the big, money-center banks are usually headed by people from close-knit, ethnic groups who have grown up together and know each other very well. They have to be able to trust each other in order to do business. There are three such groups in the United States: the Jews, the overseas Chinese, and that rarified group of Englishmen formerly known as WASPs.

When trust fails, disaster strikes. Occasionally the counterparty turns out to be untrustworthy. That describes Bernie Madoff, who sneaked off with billions of dollars. More commonly, one of the principals becomes insolvent and can't make good on his debts. The collapse of Lehman Brothers in 2008 is a good example.

So there are three jobs left for human beings in finance: risk takers (traders), salesmen, and individuals trustworthy enough to make deals on a handshake. These are all lucrative jobs. Most other jobs will more or less disappear in the New Normal.

My computer will talk to your computer.

Study Questions

1. If deflation is -1%, and the real rate of return on a diversified stock portfolio is expected to be 5.5%, what must the nominal rate of return be? Alternatively, what will be the nominal rate of return with a 2.3% inflation rate?

2. Payscale.com quotes the ROI for various colleges. We argue that the ROI depends more on you than on the college you attend. Why might that statement be true?

3. Treating college as an *investment* only applies if you are attending to advance your career. If you go to college for some other reason, then it is considered to be a *consumer good*. In your case, what fraction of your college expense can be considered an investment?

4. Will a job in the *consumer discretionary* (see chapter two) industry be better in an inflationary environment, or a deflationary one?

IF YOU DON'T GO TO COLLEGE (AND EVEN IF YOU DO)

Help Wanted: Front-Desk Manager for Large Hotel. Energetic young person needed to take full responsibility for the front desk of a large, four-star hotel. Must be personable and attractive. Needs superb people skills to handle both employees and customers. Responsible for firing and hiring, scheduling, employee training, supervision, and especially, customer satisfaction. Should have accounting experience. Will manage a staff of 30, including check-in, check-out, phone inquiries, and concierge services. Competitive salary.

College degree or equivalent required, along with 5 years relevant experience. Drug test, credit check, and criminal background check all required before employment. Please send cover letter, resume, and complete contact information for five references to Mr. Walden at ... . No phone calls please. AA/EOE

Are you depressed yet? You should be. Mr. Walden will get dozens of applications—that's dozens of people who put in considerable effort preparing that application. At best, one of them will get the job. Just as likely, somebody who already works at the hotel will be promoted to the position.

But don't get too depressed, because we just made up that ad. Indeed, in its current form it's illegal. Employers are not allowed to discriminate on age, so the request for a "young person" isn't permitted. Further, the word "attractive" might be construed as discrimination on the basis of race or ethnicity, and probably won't appear in any real ad. Still, this is a pretty good illustration of what employers are looking for.

You need to do two things. First, you need to get the job. For this your signal is very important—you need at least the "equivalent" of a college degree. What does that mean? We'll discuss that here and in the next section. Then you need to keep the job. This depends on performance—the signal fades in significance over time. We'll consider this problem later in the chapter. While these tasks overlap, they are not the same. It's useful to think about them separately.

What Employers Look For

The employer will want you to have the technical skills necessary to do the job. That could be computer programming, or nursing, or writing, or whatever. You can demonstrate this through a school transcript, through prior employment experience, by taking an exam, or by claiming expertise from a hobby.

Then the boss might be interested in some other ancillary talents you have. Perhaps he looks to hire a computer programmer, but somebody who can change the oil on the company van on the side would be helpful. The State School grad able and willing to do that might have an edge over the alum from MIT.

That's an exaggerated example, but it illustrates the point. Dan's daughter is more typical. She was hired because she can write. But the company frequently sponsors events for its subscribers, plus it also sends staff to attend other industry functions. These are important ways the firm advertises itself, and include dinners, cocktail parties, the occasional conference, etc. Of all the people who can write well, Dan's daughter got the job in part because she's attractive, fashionable, and enjoys those events. She reports that interviewees for similar positions are never hired if they're sloppily dressed. Writing is essential, but representing the company at customer events is important. Of course that never shows up in a job ad.

When you're on a job interview, consider what additional skills you have that, while they may not be advertised, might tip the balance.

Beyond skills, the most important thing an employer looks for is trustworthiness. This is an important trait that college does not signal effectively. Of course it means not stealing. More generally, the employer wants to hire good stewards of time, money, and resources. Both Dan and Tom have supervised employees who failed the trustworthy standard.

Dan once had an employee who, while technically proficient, simply couldn't get the job done. His office was a pigsty, reflecting his mental organization. He was not organized enough to manage his own time. The only way it could work is if Dan told him every day what he had to do. He couldn't be trusted with responsibility. This employee was unreliable and untrustworthy, and while it took a great deal of effort, Dan managed to eventually separate him from the firm.

The second paragraph of the job ad demonstrates the lengths that employers will take to ensure trustworthiness. Obviously, the criminal background check tries to weed out actual thieves. If you have a felony conviction, your chances of getting a job are significantly reduced. It's not that all ex-felons are unreformed crooks, but enough of them are to make employers nervous.

The drug test is intended to weed out weed (among other drugs). Even where marijuana is legal, it will probably be a long time before employers welcome habitual smokers into their businesses. That's because dope users tend to be more irresponsible than straight people. It's not that all dope users are untrustworthy, but enough of them are to make employers skittish. Very few employers will hire somebody who regularly smokes illegal drugs. If you routinely break the law in your own life, how will you behave in the workplace?

Finally, the same questions arise from the credit check. If you can't manage your own personal finances, then how can you be trusted with the firm's resources? Yeah, some people with bad credit are just victims of circumstances, as is true with some convicted felons. But that's not usually true, and few employers are willing to take the chance.

That brings up another way that student loans can bite you in the behind, even if you finish college. Especially if you default on your loans, then your bad credit rating will disqualify you for many jobs, regardless of your education. The very thing you wanted to accomplish with your degree is undone by the measures you took to get the degree. Be very careful before you default on student loans. Remember, those will never go away.

Even if you don't default on your loans, employers are still wary of people with excessive debt. People in financial difficulties are more likely to steal or cut corners. And again, if you can't manage your own resources, then can you be trusted with your employer's?

Used in extreme moderation, student loans can help you finance an education. But they are very risky. Sadly, many students use these loans like a credit card to buy clothes, restaurant meals, and other luxuries. These folks are digging themselves into lifelong poverty.

Some employers have taken to looking at applicants' social media pages. We, along with many others, find this disturbing. One silly action performed by an 18-year-old and posted on a social media site can damage your job prospects for years to come. It is in the nature of 18-year-olds to do stupid things. In ages past these could be forgotten, but in cyberspace they now live on indefinitely.

The moral is never do anything stupid—or at least don't post it on social media. But since few people can live that way (nor should they be expected to), the social conventions around social media need to change. Sites like Facebook and Twitter should be mostly off-limits to employers apart from good cause. We think the world is gradually moving in that direction—or at least we hope so.

So starting on a career means:

- Don't get arrested;
- Don't use drugs (not smoking is also a good idea);
- Stay out of debt;
- Be careful what you post on social media.

Building a Signal Without College

In Chapter 4 we listed five personality traits that graduates *signal* by finishing college. These were intelligence, diligence (work ethic), tolerance for boredom, ability to follow directions, and ability to conform. (Trustworthiness was not included because a college degree doesn't signal it.) For employers, this is like one-stop shopping—a college grad is reasonably likely to have all these traits, and she doesn't need to look more closely. So if you can graduate from college with good grades (and simply attending is not enough), then by all means do so (though not at the cost of putting yourself irretrievably in debt).

Collecting this signal is harder if you can't go to college. There is no other one-stop shop where you can demonstrate all these traits. Instead, you'll have to work hard to put them together on a resume. Further, you'll have to do better than the college grad because the employer is going to have a harder time evaluating your credentials.

Serving in the military is probably as close to a college degree as you'll ever get. It certainly hits the boredom, follow directions, and conformity buttons. With an honorable discharge, you've also demonstrated an ability to keep your word and stick with the program—signals for work ethic and trustworthiness.

But soldiers don't necessarily have to work very hard. And neither do they have to work independently. A college degree probably signals a higher level of *self-discipline* than does military service.

Dan's son joined the military right out of high school. Now at age 24, he has no debt, a perfect credit rating, and the start of a retirement account. He's certified drug-free, and is in excellent physical condition. Obviously a recent engineering grad with modest debt is going to do better, but Dan's son has more opportunities than many with college degrees. And he's certainly much better off than those who started but never finished college.

Military service as a signal of intelligence is underrated. Joining the force requires taking the ASVAB test, which is in part an IQ test. Given the competitiveness of today's military, a high score on this test is essential. But that reputation has not yet filtered down to most employers.

A steady work record is another excellent way of acquiring a signal. If you worked at McDonalds continuously for four years, you clearly have demonstrated work ethic, boredom tolerance, direction-following, and conformity. Unfortunately, this is much harder to do than it used to be. The big fast food companies operate on very tight margins, and now tightly ration the hours they give to their employees. You have to be available for 80 hours per week in order to collect 20 hours of actual work time. Thus it's very difficult to work at places like McDonalds for an extended time.

That's less true at the corner pizza parlor. If you can work at Mom's Pizza Place for several years, you've punched a lot of buttons. This is especially true if you're given responsibility for opening and/or closing the restaurant, or have assumed some management roles. This establishes you as trustworthy.

Fast food does not signal intelligence. You'll have to do that some other way. Dan's son, for example, has acquired a number of Cisco certifications in his spare time. These require studying for and then taking a test, and they prepare him for a job in information technology when he leaves the service. By doing this, he's ticked off the *self-discipline* and *intelligence* boxes. Unlike fast food workers, his military job provides him with relevant experience—that gives him an advantage. But there's nothing that prevents anybody from getting IT certs, or learning any number of other things.

Learn as much as you can. Learn how to clean the fryer, repair the grill, fix the cash register, or solve customer's problems. Take responsibility. It will pay off for you.

The person who works at a "dead-end" job for several years instead of going to college will probably not do as well as most college grads. But she will do much better than people who fail to finish college, or those who hop from job to job thinking that it doesn't matter. It does matter. There is no such thing as a "dead-end" job. You can build a career starting from anywhere.

A full-time, low-wage worker earns about $20,000/year. Assuming you can live at home, you can possibly save about $3,000/year. Over four years, you'll have accumulated $12,000, not counting interest. Put that into a retirement account at 5% real rate of return, and by age 65 you've got a nest egg worth about $110,000. By contrast, the young woman who just finished college will be $30,000 in debt.

Put another way, four years out of high school, there is a $42,000 difference in net worth between the diligent low wage worker and the college grad. By age 65 at 5% real return, that difference grows to $375,000. The college student has to make that up just to break even.

Dan has some immigrant in-laws who moved to the US when they were in their forties. They came with their (then) grade school children. The father works as an orderly in a large hospital. The mother is a foodservice worker in the cafeteria at that same hospital. Both of these are low-wage jobs with no prospect for advancement.

Now, as they approach retirement, they hold the same jobs. Undoubtedly they've gotten a few raises, and probably some benefits. They are ten years from having their house paid off, and have managed to keep themselves (mostly) out of debt. He is very handy, and they have put a lot of sweat equity into their home, increasing its value. Their children are all adults and have jobs—none of them has attended a four-year college.

Their problem, of course, is they started on their American career too late. But subtract twenty years from their ages, and look at what you can accomplish with so-called "dead-end" jobs. By age 50 you'll have a nice house in a good neighborhood free and clear, no appreciable debt, and probably a retirement account.

Keeping Your Job

Once you have the job, the signal becomes unimportant. None of your fellow employees is going to give a flying hoo-haw if you have a bachelor's degree. This is when the rubber hits the road—the signal is a promise that you can do something useful. Starting work means that you actually have to deliver.

The first thing to remember about keeping your job is that it depends more on your fellow employees and customers than it does on your boss. (In a small company your boss is probably also a fellow worker, in which case the roles are mixed.) Thus, it is the colleagues sitting next to you who need to be kept happy. And you definitely don't want to elicit any complaints from customers. Keep that in mind and you'll do fine, no matter what the boss thinks. On the other hand, if your colleagues or customers don't like you, no amount of sucking up to the boss is going to help you any.

People like to work with people they like. You have to make yourself likeable. Here are some guidelines.

1. Do your job. Don't make your colleagues do it for you. Take full responsibility for everything you're assigned. An occasional goof or oversight is forgivable, but consistently failing to complete your tasks is the fastest way to get fired.

2. After you do your own job, then help out your colleagues *in ways they want you to help*. This is not a time for one-upmanship or for showing off. If your co-worker is in any way put off by your assistance, stop meddling. On the other hand, if one of your colleagues is just swamped and can't keep up, then an extra pair of hands will be very welcome. It will repay you several-fold in the future to help them out. (However, don't get into the habit of covering for somebody who consistently can't get their job done.)

3. Follow the office rules. Take your turn bringing donuts or making coffee, if that is the office custom. Clean up after yourself.

4. Don't be high-maintenance. Keep the complaining to a minimum (there are times when you should complain). Keep your personal problems at home, or in informal settings with co-workers. People will resent having to solve your problems for you. While some of your colleagues may become friends, most of them won't.

5. Be very careful about romantic relationships in the workplace. In and of itself, romance is not a problem, but it frequently inspires intense jealousy among other people. This can lead to all kinds of problems for you.

Dress for Success

This could be item 6 on the above list, but it is sufficiently important that we put it in a separate section.

When interviewing for a job, it is almost always appropriate to wear a formal business suit. For men that means a jacket and tie. You may be overdressed, but that's much better than the other way round. It demonstrates that you're serious.

Dan once applied for a college teaching job. The interview was over the summer, when no classes were in session. His future boss arrived fresh off the tennis court in shorts and a t-shirt. Dan was dressed in a formal suit, long-sleeved shirt, and tie. It looked silly, but Dan got the job.

More important than how you dress during the interview is how you dress when you come to work. Here is the basic rule:

> *Dress in a way that is courteous to your customers and fellow employees.*

Some years ago, Tom saw a television report about a man who started his own house painting business. It was quite successful, requiring him to hire several employees. He rigidly enforced a one rule dress code: no butt cracks. If you're in somebody's house painting their woodwork or their ceiling, the last thing the customer wants to see is a butt crack. That is simply discourteous.

Dan had a student in a chemistry lab—an older fellow (thirtyish) who was making a career change to junior high school teacher. It was easy to see why his old career wasn't working out—he was a filthy slob. He wore this old sweater that you could smell from across the room. His hair, while not long, was both untrimmed and uncombed. He had some kind of scraggly beard.

There is no way any school is going to hire this fellow. Nobody wants to be around him. People work with people they like. He made himself unlikeable. Rather than going back to college, he'd have been much better off investing in soap, hot water, and laundry detergent.

You can overdo it in the other direction, too. While a suit and tie may be appropriate for the interview, it is likely not the way people dress every day in the office. If you show up in a suit and tie every day (making allowances for the first week), you will not win many friends. Your co-workers won't appreciate somebody trying to force them to spend more time and money on clothes. Your efforts to do so will be seen as discourteous.

In many cases, you dress for the customer rather than for your co-workers. A hair stylist has to have nicely cut hair, and look very clean and neat. Dan's daughter dresses fashionably for work, not necessarily because her colleagues want her to, but because there is enough interaction with customers that she needs to.

When people ask that you *dress professionally*, they are really asking you to dress with the customer in mind. Doctors and nurses do this all the time—they wear something akin to a uniform that immediately identifies them as a professional. Dan's son—in the military—also wears a uniform to work. Academic administrators—such as deans and provosts—typically wear a suit and tie to work to mark their role in the organization. This is also common among mid-level executives in other industries.

A common dress code for many workplaces is *business casual*. This is a step down from formal business wear, and is thus cheaper, more comfortable, and more flexible. At the same time, it puts an emphasis on neatness, cleanliness, and cour-tesy. It's the "no butt cracks" rule on steroids. Shorts, t-shirts, mini-skirts, and cutoffs are generally not acceptable.

Some top executives are experts at business casual. Look how Tim Cook, CEO at Apple Computer, dresses. Or similarly, observe Larry Ellison or even Bill Gates. The true masters of the art, however, are high-end salespeople. Car salesmen and real estate agents are excellent examples. If you want to see how to dress in a customer-oriented workplace, those folks are a good role model.

Case Study: Real Estate

Pundits have been predicting the demise of the real estate agent for a couple of decades now. But it hasn't happened, and we don't believe it will happen. This is one career that the New Normal hasn't changed by all that much. It's interesting to see why.

It's probably useful to go into some detail about how the real estate industry works. First, it really is a viable career path for the right person. Second, most of you will probably buy a house at some point, and the inside scoop will help you out. Finally, it's instructive to see why the real estate market hasn't changed that much—the New Normal looks pretty much like the olden days.

The details will differ from state to state and from time to time. We report on what it was like in the states where we have bought houses at one time or another (New York, Illinois, Indiana, Missouri, Wisconsin, Washington).

Suppose I (Dan) want to sell my house. I call up a real estate agent—let's call her Sara. Sara will come to my house, look around, and give me some estimate of what I can expect to get for it. Assuming I agree on an asking price, I will then sign a *listing agreement*. This contract obligates me to keep the house up for sale for some time (usually 90 days), and to pay a commission on the sales price (often 6%, though this varies widely). If I receive an offer for the asking price or higher, I am required to either sell the house or pay the commission.

Sara then becomes the *listing agent*. Because I'm paying the commission, she represents me. Her job is to sell my house for the highest possible price. Sara will have a license from the state, typically acquired by taking a class and passing a test.

Sara works for a *broker*. A real estate broker usually owns the office, and will have a number of agents working for her. She will have a broker's license, which usually requires more schooling along with experience as an agent. The broker has *fiduciary responsibility*, i.e., is responsible for handling money. At some point—perhaps only for a few minutes—the broker will be in possession of all the purchase money and the title to the property. These will be held in an *escrow account* until closing. The broker will get a share of the commission that I pay, and along with Sara she works for me.

Once Sara has the signed listing, she will go back to her office and enter it into the *multiple listing service* (MLS) database. MLS includes all houses for sale in the country. Only licensed real estate agents are allowed to put a property on to MLS. In the past, only licensed agents had access to the MLS data—it was secret knowledge. Today that data (with one crucial exception that we'll get to in a minute) is publicly available on web sites like realtor.com, zillow.com and trulia.com. You can see it for yourself.

Now, suppose that you want to buy a house. You call up your favorite real estate agent—let's call him Mark. Mark also works for a broker, but since he's with a different firm, his broker is not the same as Sara's broker. Mark and Sara both have access to the MLS listings.

Mark is usually called the *buyer's agent*, but this is very misleading. Mark will be paid from my commission, and he works for me just as much as Sara works for me. Mark works for you only in the sense that a car salesman works for you—Mark wants to find you a house that you want to buy. Until you buy the house, he earns no money, and the money he does earn depends on the sale price for the house. His financial incentives are exactly the same as Sara's.

An important point: real estate agents *always* work for the seller. Typically they refer to the seller as the *customer*, and the buyer as the *client*.

So Mark will show you a bunch of houses that you might want to buy, including mine. And here is where Mark really does have secret knowledge—information from the MLS listing that is not posted on any public website. The MLS will tell him where to find the key for the front door. A real estate agent, by virtue of having a license, has mostly unimpeded access to any house listed on the MLS.

That's why you still need a real estate agent—without Mark you'd have no easy way to get inside and look at any of the houses. It's hard to see how this essential function will ever be computerized, so real estate agents will be around for a good while yet.

A successful real estate agent can earn a good living. You have to be very personable and good at negotiation. You don't need a college degree, but in most states you're required to get a license. That will require some education, perhaps just a class or two. Having a head for numbers will be helpful.

It is not an easy job, and it's gotten harder. The number of houses sold has decreased since 2007, so that means less revenue for agents. You have to be able to take a lot of shit—people will sometimes treat you pretty badly.

Still, if you have the talent, it's a good career choice. It's not going away.

Study Questions

1. In the ad at the top of this chapter, what do you imagine the successful applicant looks like? How do you think that person dresses for work? Does that person dress primarily for customers or for fellow employees?

2. If you aspired to be the hotel's front desk manager, what skills would you need to learn that you don't have yet? What skills do you already have?

3. Again, if you wanted the front desk manager's job, what would be the next step in your life needed to make that dream a reality?

4. Answer the above three questions for a job that you really do aspire to.

5. What single thing about your appearance can you change that will make your career more successful? What can you do tomorrow that will begin to implement that change? (Losing weight is not an answer. Very few people can realistically expect to change their body physique in any permanent way.)

THE GIG ECONOMY

Dan and Tom are both tenured professors at state universities. That means we can't be fired. Most professors get tenure by age forty, and then keep the same job until they retire. Since, by federal law, college professors can't be forced into retirement, some of our colleagues keep working well into their 70s and even 80s. So we're talking about 40 years or more working for the same employer.

Your career will not be like that. Chances are, you will hold a succession of jobs over your career. Reid Hoffman (founder of LinkedIn) describes[38] them as "gigs". Each of these gigs will last two to five years before you move on to the next one. If you start your professional career at age 25, that means you'll have 10 or 12 gigs over the course of your working life.

But we're getting ahead of ourselves. Let's start by describing the "gig" economy in its most brutal form.

Day Labor

Consider the site *taskrabbit.com*. That page connects handy people with potential employers. The categories include *delivery & moving, cleaning, personal assistant*, and *handyman*. The people who do the work used to be called *rabbits*, and they typically request around $20/hour for their services.

This is much more efficient than the old *day labor* system, where a bunch of shady guys stood around on a street corner waiting for potential employers to drive by. With *taskrabbit.com*, both employees and employers are vetted. The company collects payment information up front, so the workers are guaranteed payment. Employers get a short bio, along with access to reviews of how their potential rabbit has performed on past jobs.

But all is not happy in rabbit-land. Recently Taskrabbit blew up it's business model[39] in an effort to better accommodate customers. The goal is to increase the number of completed jobs that *taskers* (the new name for *rabbits*) can accomplish, and hence the total amount of revenue. The cost is that the taskers have much less control over their work lives than before. According to Carolyn Said,[40]

> One of the workers' major beefs is lack of control over their assignments, since the system assigns tasks rather than letting them proactively seek them out.
>
> "With the bidding system I could find jobs that interested me," said Stacey Roberts-Ohr, 48, an Oakland resident who does tasks ranging from grant writing to grocery shopping. "I could acquire new skills or use my expertise. Now, I have no input on what I'm going to do; I don't get to pick my own tasks. All I'm allowed to do is describe myself in three sentences in my profile."

If Taskrabbit can increase revenue for its taskers, then the hit on worklife quality might be worthwhile. Otherwise they will lose taskers to other competing sites.

Taskrabbit.com is an example of the *sharing economy*. At its essence, the *sharing economy* eliminates the middleman. Back in the day (if you didn't want to hang out on a street corner somewhere), cleaning houses required joining some sort of agency. The latter would advertise in the Yellow Pages (anybody remember those?), or in the classified ads of the local newspaper.

Further, a good agency acquired a reputation for honest and reliable service. Since potential customers usually had no way of evaluating the help in advance, they had to trust the agency to do the vetting for them. The agency hired people the old-fashioned way—the house cleaners worked for them as employees.

This all added to the expense of cleaning services, known as *transaction costs*. These cost real money, and often made it impossible for a potential housecleaner to work independently. The agency had to have staff, telephones, accountants, and the like. It probably added 50% or more to the hourly cost of getting your house cleaned.

Technology eliminates many of these transaction costs. Taskrabbit still does initial vetting—they won't sign up a new employee without establishing that person's identity, doing a criminal background check, and an interview. They also provide insurance for their customers. All the other agency functions are fully computerized: scheduling, payments, assessments, etc. Nobody needs to answer the phone. Most of the savings are passed on to the consumer.

The most important aspect the *sharing economy* is the public reviews. Customer reviews of their tasker are posted on the website for all to see. If a tasker does not maintain a sufficiently high rating, he is discontinued. The reviews hold the tasker *accountable* in a way that the agency employee wasn't. Customers are much more likely to get the service they have contracted for.

It is also possible for the taskers to rate the customers. While the taskers complain that those are not made available to the them, no doubt they have some effect. Misbehaving customers are probably banned from the system.

We checked for taskers available for house cleaning in a New York zip code. The lead candidate presented to us, a young lady, has a Masters degree in fine arts. As we have said before, one can build a career from anywhere, and there is nothing wrong with house cleaning—it is an honorable job. Further, her fine arts background can help, as from her self-description she is obviously aware. Home decorating is a possible, value-added addition. But what's with the Masters degree? She is over-educated and under-skilled. We hope she has no student loan debt, for otherwise she has sentenced herself to a life of poverty.

A new competitor to taskrabbit is a startup called *WunWun. com*[41] that advertises "free delivery from your favorite places." If, for example, you want carry-out from your favorite Chinese restaurant, just call up WunWun and they'll buy it for you and deliver it at no extra charge (you pay only for the food). Likewise, if your light bulb burned out or your printer just ran out of ink, WunWun can buy you a replacement and deliver it for free. (For the moment, the service is only available in New York.)

WunWun's *helpers* ride around on bicycles and are not paid by the company. Instead, they rely on tips—WunWun suggests that experienced helpers can earn $20/hour. WunWun hopes to earn money by getting discounts from vendors (that will not be passed on to the customer), and by distributing advertising flyers along with the deliveries. (In its initial incarnation, WunWun wanted a cut of tip money as well, i.e., helpers had to pay them for the privilege of working there. But they've dropped that.)

Wow! Welcome to the New Normal.

While Taskrabbit and WunWun facilitate in-person, casual employment, *fiverr.com*[42] makes connections for people who work via the Internet. The categories included graphic design, online marketing, writing & translation, and programming & tech, among other categories.

Fiverr.com offers services that can be shipped over the Internet—thus it isn't looking for bicycle messengers. It organizes tasks by what it calls "gigs." Unlike Mr. Hoffman's use of the word, these are very short-term arrangements. A single gig costs $5, of which *Fiverr* keeps $1. A vendor may charge multiple gigs for a single job.

For example, we are interested in copy-editing. Danielle[43] will copy-edit 1000 words for one gig ($5). Copy-editing a 100 page novel (25,000 words) will cost $125—a relatively low rate. She has a very high rating—4.9 out of 5—so presumably she does a good job.

Distressingly, if you go to the writing or C++ programming vendors, many vendors offer to do your school homework for you. This fellow[44] looks to make a pretty good living at it.

Neither the writers nor the C++ programmers seem to make much more per hour than the house cleaners. Admittedly, many of the programmers are from poorer countries, where $20/hour will go a long way. But don't let anybody tell you that majoring in computer science is a certain route to riches. That only works if you are *good* at it.

Another name for the *sharing economy* could be the *rotten tomatoes economy*, after the popular movie reviews site. In this new world, everything depends on customers' ratings. Bad word of mouth results in bad box office—on steroids.

The Gig Economy

So while the short-term, day-labor gigs just described might be a place to start a career, they're probably not the way you want to lead your life. So let's return to Reid Hoffman's larger definition of the term—a *gig* is a period of two to five years during which you work on a project for a company. After that, you'll move on to another project, likely with a different company.

Today, you and your boss both work on a project for Company X. Tomorrow you may both work on something else for

Company Y—except for that project you might be the boss. Both of you will be independent contractors in some sense, moving from project to project. Since you're both in the same business, it's no surprise that occasionally your careers will cross.

In Mr. Hoffman's vision, the connecting link between these projects will be LinkedIn. That's the place where all the expertise will be recorded. You, your boss, and many other people will all be linked together, able to find each other quickly and easily. It will be easy to put together a team for any project.

LinkedIn will be the on-line store of your *reputation*. You will be known by the company you keep. Your reputation can't be evaluated like they do at Taskrabbit. None of your LinkedIn friends is going to award you "stars" or give you a "bad" review. So the star system isn't going to work—at least not directly.

Lets suppose you work for The Widget Company on their *improved widget project*. The work is finished in 18 months, six months ahead of schedule. This is mostly due to your diligence and smarts—everybody who worked on the project knows that.

Accordingly, your colleagues will all send requests to join your LinkedIn circle. You'll have lots of friends and acquaintances— people who know you professionally and can vouch for your skills. Through your friends shall you be known—having a big LinkedIn circle is the same as getting high star rating.

Conversely, let's suppose you never got enthusiastic about the *improved widget project*. Indeed, the company decided to dispense with your services eight months into the effort. Not only will you not get many "friend" requests from your former colleagues, you'll probably find the your offers to "friend" them are ignored. Your circle is going to be much smaller—and accordingly your future opportunities greatly restricted.

LinkedIn's problem is to ensure that you can't fake your identity. Unlike Facebook or other social media sites, they work to make sure you really are who you say you are. That means your reputation follows you for the rest of your career. As you move further along in your career, your future is more and more in the hands of people whom you worked with years ago, or perhaps never met at all. This is both good and bad news. On the one hand, it's going to make it harder to get a fresh start. In the old days you could hide or downplay the sour notes on your resume—that's a whole lot harder to do now. Your reputation is going to follow you around no matter what you do.

On the other hand, we've talked a lot about *signal*. LinkedIn proposes to let you create a signal that's much cheaper than going to college. If LinkedIn can demonstrate your work record, then your college career becomes unimportant, except insofar as it gave you essential skills.

LinkedIn, if it accomplishes its goals, becomes highly disruptive. In principle, it puts colleges out of business. It will give people like you an opportunity to establish a reliable signal without having to spend four to six years in college first. If they can pull this off, it will be of enormous benefit, not only to you, but to society as a whole.

We have mentioned before that companies like Google are putting less emphasis on college credentials when hiring. Indeed, it looks to us that the technology industry is already succumbing to the new LinkedIn model. Whether and how fast this spreads to other industries remains to be seen.

The LinkedIn model appears to work very well for jobs that really are project related, e.g., computer science and engineering jobs. On the other hand, the nursing station at the hospital has to be staffed all the time—that job doesn't really fit into the "project" mold. So we predict that LinkedIn will be less important for those kinds of jobs.

Birth of a Salesman

The LinkedIn model will work well for a lot of people. People who are outgoing and gregarious will thrive—if they can maintain their reputation. To work successfully in the LinkedIn world, you'll need to develop a specialized niche in a supply chain, and you need to be a person other people want to work with. Then your career depends on how well you can market yourself. How big is your network? How public are your successes? Can you schmooze?

Dan's sister has made a career in Hollywood, working behind the camera. Hers is a very specialized skill. Her career mostly preceded LinkedIn, but she nevertheless epitomizes the kind of career a LinkedIn worker can have. Her marketing depends entirely on her network—people with whom she has worked in the past, and even others who compete with her for the same jobs (too much work gets spread around). She's earned a living because 1) she's good at her job and 2) she's sufficiently gregarious to get the gigs.

Her gigs are not the day labor sort described in the last section, nor are they the 2-5 year-long projects that Mr. Hoffman models. Instead, they are day-long to months-long engagements for a commercial or movie. The crew for these projects is put together through the network—and increasingly that's mediated through LinkedIn.

Put bluntly, Dan's sister is a good saleslady. She's just selling her own abilities and talents, but there's no reason why other things can't be sold the same way. That is, if you can sell yourself and your abilities, then there's no reason why you can't sell any number of other things as well.

Salespeople will do really well in the New Normal. While the cashier can be automated, the salesman can't be. The job of a salesman is to find solutions for customers.

A few years back, Dan and his wife rather urgently needed a used car. The salesman asked us a few questions and then immediately took us to the back of the lot and showed us exactly what we wanted at a price we could afford. Yeah—we shopped around at other dealers for the rest of the day, but later that afternoon we went back and bought that car.

No webpage will ever replace that salesman. So much of what we wanted was intangible, or at least not easy to articulate. It wasn't like we could've gone to webpage and clicked off a bunch of boxes. We needed not only his expertise and knowledge about what was on the lot on that day, but also his ability to understand what we really wanted.

Likewise, we've had similar experiences with real estate agents. We've already mentioned that they refer to the buyers as *clients*—and that's a good word. A skilled realtor will work hard to find the clients the house they want to buy. She has to know both her clients and the market very well in order to do that.

Dan remembers once having a really bad agent. She tried the hard sell—we were pressured to buy every house we looked at, regardless if it worked for us or not. Needless to say, we got ourselves another agent. Selling people something they don't want is not a successful strategy.

Lots of jobs will morph into sales positions. Dan, for example, increasingly sees his job as a chemistry professor at convincing the students to spend time doing the homework. That's really the only way they'll learn chemistry. Increasingly, apart from lab work, chemistry instruction will move online. Then the function of the live professor will be exclusively sales. We will do our best to motivate students to watch the lectures, take the quizzes, and do the homework. That's a different job from what professors do today.

As production and services become automated, the remaining job for humans will be to guide customers through the cornucopia of products out there. Humans will have to make the customer happy—that's called being a salesman.

On the other hand, people who are more reserved or introverted will not do so well. Your career will be more difficult. Though Tyler Cowen has suggested that people who fall somewhere along the autism spectrum may do very well. They'll be superb programmers and engineers.

If you fall off the LinkedIn ladder, it may become increasingly difficult to get back on it again. If you're less successful on a gig, the hit to your reputation becomes increasingly permanent.

Case Study: Musicians

Dan's father was an oboist for a symphony orchestra early in his career. As it didn't really pay enough to support a family, he gave it up and moved onto another profession.

Because of that heritage, and consistent with his age and status as an academic, Dan remains a fan of classical music. While he listens to all kinds of music, his "comfort listening" (after a hard day at work) is Mozart and Haydn piano sonatas and concertos.

His favorite performer is Alfred Brendel, a specialist in the music of Mozart and Beethoven. If you listen to classical music at all, you may have heard of Mr. Brendel. He's probably among the most famous pianists of all time.

Music is an excellent example of a *winner-take-all* market. If you're going to pay money for music, surely you will download or stream the most famous, very best pianist such as Mr. Brendel. Why would you settle for second best? The world's second best pianist may be almost as good, but given the money you're spending, you will go for the top person with the best reputation.

Basketball is another *winner-take-all* profession. There are lots of excellent basketball players out there, but the only ones most people watch are the few hundred in the NBA. None of the remaining tens of thousands can earn a living at the sport.

There are lots of *winner-take-all* professions: movie stars, book authors, famous professors. But music is among the most extreme—in an age of ubiquitous downloading and streaming, the second best pianist doesn't stand a chance. Mr. Brendel sells way more than his share of downloads and CDs, probably more than the next hundred pianists combined. That's pretty good for an 83-year-old guy.

Mr. Brendel lived at just the right time. Pianists before him did not have access to good recording technology. They made a bunch of scratchy records that only connoisseurs like. And pianists who came after him can't make a name for themselves— they permanently live in Mr. Brendel's shadow. (There are a few exceptions: a relatively young pianist named Simone Dinnerstein has done a superb job packaging Bach.)

Of course, the same trend applies to other kinds of music, such as hip-hop or jazz. After all, if you can download jazz pianist Oscar Peterson (undoubtedly one of the greats of all time), why would you bother purchasing a track from Tom George?

Tom George? Does that name ring a bell? Oh yeah—he's one of the authors of this book, who doubles as a university president. But he's trained as a classical musician who moved into jazz in his early years. He's not as good as Oscar Peterson, but if the world were fair he'd earn at least half as much money as his more esteemed colleague.

As it turns out, Tom earns almost nothing from selling recordings—probably not enough for a cup of coffee at Starbucks. Nobody except for his personal friends is going to take a chance on him instead of Oscar Peterson. Rather than *winner-take-all*, he's among the *loser-gets-nothing* crowd, which includes almost all living musicians.

So if you intend to make a career as a famous recording artist, please think again. You will almost certainly fail—the only exception being if you are very good *and* very lucky. Or perhaps you have some other talent or charisma, such as the famous violinist Sarah Chang, who is not only an excellent musician but also an attractive woman. Her glamorous persona sells recordings.

So, a lot of people interested in music recognize this. Instead of majoring in music performance, they study something like *music business* or *sound recording technology*. Indeed, these may qualify as *fad majors*—student interest greatly exceeds job opportunities. The New Normal is not kind to these professions—they are increasingly automated out of existence. Recording equipment is now sufficiently cheap that individuals can afford it, and given the very low income it doesn't pay to do much more than that.

Does this mean music is purely a hobby—that it's impossible to earn a living? Absolutely not! While it is no longer possible to make a career as a recording artist (except for the lucky few), live performance is still very much a possibility. No computer can do that, and at his advanced age Mr. Brendel isn't in the running.

We've been talking about the *gig economy*. It may be that musicians invented that word—they've been playing gigs for a long time. Tom, unsuccessful as a recording artist, plays as many gigs as he has time for—in coffee shops, private parties, and in churches. Were he a real pro, he undoubtedly could scratch out a living as a performer. It's a hard life, but if you really love music, are good at it, and have some showbiz skills, go for it.

Some performers earn income as street musicians. This is particularly true in places that attract lots of tourists, such as New York or New Orleans. On a side street in Lower Manhattan, Dan encountered an *a capella* quartet singing old rock 'n roll songs. They'd picked the location for the acoustics—it was not a major thoroughfare. They had no instruments, no microphone, and no music stands. All they had was undiluted, raw talent. They'd attracted a large crowd, partially blocking traffic, and were making money like nobody's business.

There's a fine line between street musicians and beggars. But the best ones clearly add value to the tourist experience.

Study Questions

1. We've distinguished gig economy jobs from other kinds of jobs, such as nursing. Think of three examples from each category that are not mentioned in the text. Explain your answer.

2. What are some of the advantages and disadvantages of building a career in the gig economy?

3. Is the career you're thinking about likely to be part of the gig economy? Why or why not?

4. Dan's dad tried to make a living as an oboist in a symphony orchestra. It didn't work for him. Would he be more likely to succeed today? Why or why not?

THE ORGANIZATION
MAN

In his younger days, Dan drove a taxicab in Chicago for several years. When he started, Chicago's Checker Cab company manufactured the Checker Marathon taxicab.[45] Of course, if you make your own cars, you have to hire your own mechanics and run your own garages, along with gas stations. The company had dispatchers and its own radio shop (there were no cell phones in those days). The drivers were all unionized and got paid a commission on the fare (in addition to tips).

There was a huge overhead cost in running Checker Cab company: manufacturing, car sales (to taxi companies around the world), maintenance, hiring, etc. It involved a big capital investment. The company protected that investment in two ways. One, they sought protection from the mob, and second, they sought protection from local government.

The mob connection was broken up years ago, but the government connection remains. In Chicago, New York, and many other large cities, you can't drive a cab without a *medallion*. The medallion is permission from the city government to operate a taxicab. Taxi medallions in New York City traded for as much than a million dollars a few years ago. Since the city (at least in New York) offers far fewer medallions than necessary to serve the market, owning a medallion was fairly literally a license to print money.

So taxi companies could afford to hire all those people: the accountants, mechanics, gas pump jockeys, dispatchers, etc.

There were lots of those people—perhaps as many as there were cab drivers. But the customer never saw them. Those folks all worked in the background, nominally for the purpose of keeping the cabs on the road, but also because the medallion-enabled monopoly produced enough cash to make the payroll.

Whyte and Coase

All those people—the people the customer never sees and who produce no direct revenue for the company—we call *organization men*. *Organization men* (which today, includes women) are essentially overhead—an expense.

The term comes from a book by William Whyte, *The Organization Man*, published in 1956.[46] He wasn't talking about cab companies—his interest was the white collar worker, who in his day was just beginning to move to the suburbs. The thesis seems quaint today—those faceless men in suits and ties who lived conformist lives in meaningless suburbs, working for huge bureaucracies. Oh how we miss those days, when with a college degree you could get a secure, well-paying, white-collar job with *General Motors* or *Hilton Hotels*.

What happened to the *organization man*?

Around the same time (1960) the American economist Ronald Coase (1910-2013) asked a very strange question: Why are there firms? Why, for example, are there big companies like *General Motors*, or huge hotel chains like *Hilton Hotels*? Everybody took the existence of these corporate behemoths for granted—as probably you do even today. Leave it to an economist to ask the silly question.

The question came up because economists have always believed that the market price is the most efficient price. If widgets are too expensive, people won't buy them and the widget company won't make any money. On the other hand, if widgets are priced too cheaply, then the store will run out of widgets. There will be disappointed people who can't get any.

The correct price is the market price—where supply meets demand. That is the price at which there will be no unhappy consumers (whoever wants a widget can buy one), and the widget company can sell all its widgets. The market price is the price that maximizes revenue for the widget company (benefiting both employees and shareholders), and maximizes benefit to consumers (the largest number of consumers will get a widget without the stores running out).

But a big company like *General Motors* doesn't work that way. They manufacture many of their parts in-house. That is, rather than using the efficient market, they bureaucratically determine how many of a given auto part they should make, and how much it should cost. Likewise with labor—it would be much better for GM to hire labor on the open market by using a site like *taskrabbit*. That would match job seekers with positions at GM with maximum efficiency.

General Motors doesn't do that. Instead, today it has 219,000 employees who are on steady payroll, paid whether they are needed or not on a given day. Why? There is no way that is efficient, and therefore does not maximize benefits for either the customer or the shareholder.

So Mr. Coase asked the question: Why doesn't GM reduce its payroll to, say, 10 people, and buy everything else off the open market as needed? Why are there firms?

Mr. Coase's answer to this question was *transaction costs*. Suppose GM wanted to hire an expert in fuel injection technology for a given day. It would have to advertise the position, vet the applicants in some way, and then hire that person for an eight-hour shift. The employee, meanwhile, needs to fly up from his home in Houston in order to do the job. All this imposes costs completely incidental to making cars, and together they more than eliminate any benefit from using the open market.

Accordingly, once GM has found somebody expert in fuel injection technology, it just keeps him on the payroll indefinitely, avoiding the transaction costs. Saving on transaction costs more than makes up for the cost and inefficiency of the bureaucracy.

In Mr. Coase's formulation, firms will grow until the costs of bureaucracy equal the savings in transaction costs.

So what's different about the New Normal? The Internet reduces transaction costs, and in doing so it reduces the size of firms. In terms of number of employees, companies are getting smaller and smaller. The *organization man* is disappearing.

Robots

General Motors' global employment peaked in 1979 at 618,000 employees. They have *outsourced* a large fraction of their production. During the 1980s and 90s, much of that was moved to Mexico and China. By buying parts on the open market overseas, GM was able to reduce prices and (more significantly) hugely improve the quality of their product.

Beginning in the aughts, and especially since 2007, manufacturing is increasingly automated. GM, famously, was among the first to begin using robots. That's because its unionized workforce was very expensive, and the payoff for investment in automation was substantial. More recently, automation has become cheaper and cheaper, and robots are going more and more mainstream. They now even use them in the commercials.[47]

The result is that labor costs are no longer the significant expense for manufacturing. Thus there is less benefit to locating in a low-wage country. Other considerations dominate: proximity to markets, cost of electricity, availability of the skilled labor still required, and cost of raw materials. The United States frequently excels in all respects, and thus manufacturing has been moving back to the US in a major way. The robots are all getting good jobs.

And some people are, too. Robots require constant maintenance, repair, and programming. These are the skilled manufacturing jobs that pay well today. They often don't require a college degree, but they do require some kind of training and an apprenticeship. While we take all talk of labor shortages with a grain of salt, it is likely that there is today a shortage of the technically-trained personnel needed to run a modern factory.

Back in the 1990s, Dan took a tour of a peanut butter plant. The company made generic brand peanut butter for grocery stores across North America, each asking for its own recipe.

The production line was completely automated. Human beings played only supporting roles. The boss was the chef—he was responsible for making sure the correct recipe was used for any given run. This was mostly a matter of opening and closing valves, changing the ratio of ingredients. Then forklift drivers took bags of peanuts off of trucks and delivered them to the line. The peanuts were dumped—shells and all—into a giant hopper. Every part of the peanut was used. The parts not used for peanut butter—the shells and the paper-like cover on each nut—were separated to be sold or used elsewhere.

A quality control team sampled the product at various points along the line to make sure everything was coming out right. And an engineer was on duty to fix any problems that might arise. More forklift drivers took the boxes packed with peanut butter jars to waiting trucks for shipment. Once per week the line was shut down, and all employees from all three shifts got together to clean the whole shebang thoroughly from top to bottom.

That was in the 1990s. Today, the process is probably done with fewer moving parts. Instead of valves, the chef likely sits at a computer terminal. The forklifts may be automated, as may be the quality control operation. Even the cleaning can be automated. So, today it's likely that fewer people can produce even more peanut butter at a yet cheaper price.

With fewer employees, the Human Resources office can get smaller. Fewer accountants are needed, as are fewer lawyers (there won't be as many injuries). A crew of five doesn't need a full-time manager. The *organization man* just got laid off.

While we are on the topic of robotics, let us mention a company whose headquarters and IT operations are located on Tom's university campus: Express Scripts. With annual sales exceeding $100 billion, this Fortune 20 company founded in 1986 is the largest pharmacy benefit manager in the country. Right next to campus, they have a building that relies on robotics to process pharmaceuticals for home delivery by mail. Their philosophy is to provide access to pharmaceuticals of the highest accuracy and lowest possible price to as many people as possible. While they partner with pharmacies that dispense medicine in the store (instead of by mail), they feel that the future roles of pharmacists will look different from today, where the more routine tasks such as counting pills into a bottle will be done through robotics. Dan thinks many of those pharmacists are likely to be laid off.

The Organization Man Goes Away

You can watch the *organization man* disappear in real time, today. Let's go back to the taxi business and consider the upstart company, *Uber*.

Uber (along with competing companies such as *Lyft* and *Sidecar*) lets people use their own cars as a taxicab. That completely eliminates any fleet management. No cab company needs to own more than one car.

Uber drivers buy gas at the cheapest gas station they can find. Unlike the old days, when company bureaucrats purchased gasoline in bulk, the current model is much more cost-effective. Likewise, gone are the company mechanics. Drivers save money by purchasing at the market price.

Uber dispatches cabs using a mobile phone app. The process is completely automated. Gone are the folks who used to answer the phone, and gone is the quaint and charming radio dispatch lingo. *Uber*, from their headquarters in San Francisco, can in principle dispatch a cab to your doorstep anywhere in the world.

All of the *organization men* that Checker Cab Company used to employ are rendered redundant, replaced by a big computer and few dozen people sitting in an office in San Francisco. The traditional cab companies are still hiding behind the medallion, claiming that *Uber* is illegal. But their battle is lost — the laws will soon be changed.

Hotel chains have a similar problem. A new outfit called *Airbnb* allows for individuals to rent out spare bedrooms in their houses. It's basically an automated reservation system and payment protocol that connects people who need a place to stay with people who have a spare room.

Think about all the money that saves. No need to tie up a lot of expensive real estate downtown. There are zillions of people out there with spare rooms all over town. And once again, most of the lawyers, accountants, and managers will be laid off, as will all the reservations agents. The only people who still have a job in the *Airbnb* world are folks who interact directly with the customer — the host and the person who cleans the room.

While traditional cab companies will all go out of business, that's probably not true for large hotels. Conventions, for example, require that people all stay close to the meeting venue, and that is much easier to manage through a hotel. People in transit may find the roadside Holiday Inn more convenient than an *Airbnb* location somewhere in town. And fancy resorts that serve fine food on the beach will always have a place. So there will remain a market for hotels—but it will be a smaller market than they have today. Like the cab companies, they're complaining.

So here's the bottom line for you. If you're proposing a career as an *organization man*, your job may be at risk. An *organization man* is anybody who doesn't provide direct value-added service to the customer. If you don't want to drive a cab, you'll never work for a cab company. If you don't own a spare bedroom, it's a lot harder to work for a hotel.

Jennifer, our database administrator for a large hospital in the city, is an *organization man*. She provides no direct benefit to the patient. In this she is different from the nurse, whom the patient sees every day. Database administration can be contracted out at market prices. A hospital that can save money by getting rid of their database administrator will certainly do so. The patient will never know the difference.

Careers to avoid include lawyers, accountants, managers, secretaries, or any back-office personnel. Those jobs won't all disappear—the world will always need some *organization men*. But increasingly their services are going to be contracted out. You'll have to work as a freelancer.

Climbing the corporate ladder just isn't what it used to be.

Entrepreneurs

It's hard to know who the boss is anymore.

If you "work" for *Uber*, that means you own your own car and you manage your own time. For legal reasons, if for no other, *Uber* denies that you're an employee. Indeed, quite the opposite—it's just as logical to say that they work for you rather than you work for them. You are employing *Uber* to handle dispatch and payment services for you. *Uber* certainly understands it that way—they view the drivers as their customers, and treat them accordingly. (Dan thinks it's probably a whole lot better to "work" for *Uber* than for the old Checker Cab Company.)

Similar arguments can be made for *taskrabbit*, *WunWun* and *Airbnb*. The last one requires that you own a spare room that you can rent out. *WunWun* doesn't even give you a paycheck — you live on tips. These organizations serve as marketplaces — where buyer and seller can get together. They are certainly not employers in any traditional sense. In modern lingo, they're often called *platforms*.

The *platforms* have probably taken Ronald Coase's idea to the ultimate limit. The transaction costs are covered by a fee, and therefore there's no reason to have a firm anymore. Everybody offering services on these *platforms* is a sole-proprietor entrepreneur.

Still, it's probably worthwhile to consider entrepreneurship in the more traditional sense, namely owning your own business. Here is the basic difference between an entrepreneur and an employee:

- An *employee* only invests her own human capital. She puts up no other money or resource for the business.

- An *entrepreneur* invests not only in human capital, but also in other resources necessary to conduct the business. Typically, she puts up *financial capital*, aka money.

By this definition, *Uber* drivers and *Airbnb* hosts are entrepreneurs. The driver needs to have a car that meets specs. And to sell on *Airbnb*'s platform, you need a room or an apartment to rent. These all involve money above and beyond human capital. These people are true *entrepreneurs*.

The *Airbnb* host illustrates another feature of the entrepreneur. Many hosts are renting out their second home or vacation home. For example, Dan's wife has a cousin who lives in England but owns a vacation home in Florida. For much of the year they rent it out on *Airbnb* (except when they're using it themselves). Obviously they can't fly to Florida every time the place needs to be cleaned, so they *hire* somebody to do that job for them. Thus they are an *employer*. They may very well hire that person off the gig economy, perhaps using a site like *taskrabbit*.

And that brings us round full circle. The *organization man* hasn't really gone away. Instead, he's become an entrepreneur. The entrepreneur is the fellow who hires the accountant, the cleaner, the mechanic, and the programmer. Many of these people will be hired off the gig economy, but somebody needs to *organize* what they do. That's the job of the entrepreneur.

So if you like putting deals together, and are good at assembling a team of people to do a task, then by all means you should become an *organization man*, nowadays an *entrepreneur*. Unlike the *organization man* of old, you'll have to put up your own money and be your own salesman. It won't be the cushy, corner-office job that Grandpa once had with *General Motors*, but it will potentially be very satisfying and rewarding.

Entrepreneurship is a worthy profession. There are a lot of books out there that will help you get started. You do need to have the right personality for it.

Case Study: College Professor

Today's colleges are increasingly obsolete institutions, out of sync with the New Normal. They invest a huge amount in bureaucracy. Along with many other government agencies, the *organization man* is still the big man on campus.

Colleges still manage dormitories, and this in a day when not even the large hotel chains are efficient operators. Campuses in-source the maintenance of their physical plant. We still have a mailroom, a telecommunications office, a parking office, a police department, and until recently we managed our own e-mail servers.

All of these services can be had more cheaply at market rates. Ronald Coase's criterion—that bureaucracy is justified only when transaction costs are higher—has long since been violated. It is only for political reasons that colleges still provide all these extraneous services.

So, perhaps it is not surprising that professors also spend a lot of time as *organization men*. The ostensible purpose is to *manage the curriculum*. In the past, it all made sense. When Dan first started his career in the 1980s, it was very reasonable. That's because the transaction costs of doing it differently were prohibitive.

The premise is that the faculty are experts in their disciplines, and also are knowledgeable about what students need to know for a career. Thus the faculty are the ones who determine what classes are required for a particular degree. As circumstances changed, the degree requirements also changed. For example, in recent decades, computer proficiency has become a formal part of the curriculum.

In practice, the faculty vote on the curriculum. While they usually don't have sole authority, their word is pretty powerful, and few college administrators will dare to override them. To their credit, the faculty take this responsibility very seriously. The result is a series of committees, long agendas, and endless meetings, all of which take up a lot of time. As much as one third of faculty time is taken up with this enterprise.

The faculty are expert in their disciplines, and therefore they will always have a say in what you learn. If you want to study chemistry, for example, Dan and Tom know more than you do. You'd be well advised to listen to us. But even there, it's been a long time since we've worked at anything besides teaching college. Dan last worked for a pharmaceutical firm in 1985. He knows very little about the technology and processes they use today.

Here's the rub. In the relatively slowly changing world of the last Century, just by virtue of experience, faculty knew something about the world of work. But the New Normal is completely different. It is almost totally outside the experience of most tenured professors. They're stuck in a sixty-year-old timewarp, about as far removed from the world you are entering as it is possible to be.

So the premise—that faculty understand what you need to know for your career—is just flat out wrong. They know less than you do. Or, as we have already put it: *nobody can predict the future, but you know more about your own future than anybody else*—certainly more than most college faculty.

So, we predict that college professors will gradually lose their control over the curriculum. That power will devolve to students and their future employers. For example, it may be that your LinkedIn reputation (which will certainly include what you learn in school) will loom much larger than the rules laid down by faculty. Or, possibly, we'll end up with a *just-in-time* model, where you'll take classes on a *need-to-know* or *want-to-know* basis.

Degrees will be less important. Skills are what it's all about.

Colleges will always exist. There will always be human professors, though probably fewer of them. Students will spend less time on campus, and more of their coursework will be delivered online. Faculty will work in an environment that is more similar to where you will be working—they'll be freelancers in the gig economy. They won't have landline telephones, desktop computers, or even offices. Classrooms will look more like a bookstore or like Starbucks. The lecture hall is fading away. Most professors probably won't get paid very much, but a few of them will be millionaires. Like music, it will become in part a winner-take-all profession.

And they won't be spending a lot of time sitting around in meetings.

Study Questions

1. Consider the job ad for the position of hotel manager at the top of Chapter 8. How might that job change in light of this chapter?

2. *Purchasing Agent* is a popular job title. Will this person be more important or less important in the New Normal?

3. Many college students, especially those majoring in liberal arts disciplines, aspire to be college professors. Is this a realistic goal? Knowing what you now know, do you still want to be a college professor? Why or why not?

THE WORLD IS NOT YOUR OYSTER

Let's begin by summarizing the lessons we've learned in this book.

1) Look at the big picture. Understand how your job relates to the consumer. Study the underlying economics of the industry you're in, and understand your role in the process.

2) *Anything that can be automated, eventually will be.* It's hard to predict the technological future, but we discussed some kinds of jobs that are likely to survive. Those include jobs that:

i) require sophisticated use of the five senses. The short-order cook will likely be automated, but the skilled chef will always have a job.

ii) provide person-to-person emotional support. Real estate agents provide a true service that cannot be computerized. Similarly, while large parts of the teacher's job can be computerized, some core piece of it will always remain human.

iii) require a true understanding of the reasons for the rules (as opposed to just memorizing the rules). Human lawyers won't do discovery anymore, but the judge in a criminal trial will always be a human being.

iv) have a legal or financial stake in the outcome. No robot can ever sign a contract or be arrested. Only people can buy and sell shares, or pay debts or taxes. Financial institutions will always have human beings as their principals.

v) generate new content, i.e., text, pictures, events, movies, etc., that people want to consume. Computers can already generate content, but almost by definition that stuff is boring. Only people can entertain or enlighten other people.

3) Be good at what you do. You have to be good enough to earn a living. If you want to work as a pro-basketball player, you need to be really, really good. The bar for being a real estate agent is much lower (though still substantial). Be realistic about your abilities. Remember Bryan Caplan's advice: *If you're doing something hard and not being very successful, you can either try harder, or you can do something easier.* In many cases the best advice is to do something easier — something that you're good at.

4) Go to college only if you're good at it. At very least you need to graduate — otherwise college is pretty much a waste of time. But even that may not be sufficient. Students who struggle through chemistry, for example, with a C average are probably not going to be working as chemists. Those students might be better off doing something easier.

5) Whether or not you go to college, make sure you learn a skill. Computers know things, but they can't as easily do things. Learn how to do something that's not easily automated. See point 2).

6) *Save Money Now.* The dollar you save today will be the most valuable dollar you ever have. Your future happiness may well depend more on how much money you save rather than on your career.

By the same token, avoid going into debt. We won't say *never* take out student loans — if you're Albert Einstein, and a hard worker besides, it might pay off. But most of you should probably not borrow money to go to college. If you can't afford to go to school, don't go right away, go someplace cheaper, or don't go at all. Digging yourself into a hole before age 20 is not a good idea.

7) Be careful with your reputation. Keep your word. Do your job. The *signal* you earn by going to college is just a shorthand for your reputation. There's no point in going to college and then blowing it by failing at your first job. Reread Chapter 7 about how to earn a signal without going to college. Those are the personality traits you want to advertise if you can.

Similarly, make yourself attractive to your workmates and your customers. You do this by your behavior, by your demeanor, and by how you dress. People like to work with people they like.

Pay attention to social media. Don't post anything that will disqualify you from employment. LinkedIn (or some site like it) may play a much more important part in your life than it does now. It might become the store of your reputation, possibly replacing the signal from going to college. Be as careful as you can about what appears on LinkedIn.

8) The gig economy is both an opportunity and a threat. It provides you with opportunities to market your product or service worldwide. Potentially, you can make a lot more money. On the other hand, it reduces previously well-paid careers to low-wage labor, as is happening today with college professors and lawyers.

9) If you work as an *organization man*, there is a big chance you'll be working in the gig economy. Lawyers that hang out their shingles have long been doing gigs. But that trend is spreading: computer programmers, graphic designers, database administrators, accountants, etc. The Internet allows for skills to be hired as needed for short-term

projects. Job security and long-term employment are becoming much harder to get.

Entrepreneurship is a job that will never be computerized. If you have the talent for it, it is probably one of the very best options around.

So now comes the unvarnished truth: your work life will probably be less pleasant than that of your parents or grandparents. You will work harder (though not necessarily longer) at less interesting jobs, for lower pay. You'll have less job security and fewer opportunities for advancement. In a word, it sucks.

Your parents and grandparents could work for a large corporation as an accountant or as a lawyer. Again, while that may still be possible for some of you, the *organization man* is fading away. The corporate ladder is getting shorter and shorter—there are fewer opportunities there.

Your parents and grandparents could become tenured college professors. While that may still be possible for the select few, for most people this is no longer a viable career track.

More of you are going to be employed in the gig economy. By definition, those jobs are insecure and come with no benefits. You'll have to live by your wits.

Your job will be more boring, require more sucking-up, be less intellectual, and put a premium on smiley-faced, customer-first friendliness. That's the New Normal. You won't enjoy it very much because it will feel like you're losing ground.

But you are not.

Because, while prices and wages will both go down (in real terms, after adjusting for inflation), prices will go down faster. That's because robots essentially work for free. So, even though you're only earning chump change, that's a lot more than what the robot gets. The robot sells all those products and services to human beings for nearly nothing—only the cost of raw materials and electricity.

Against almost-free, your chump change will go a long way—you'll live high on the hog. Indeed, we predict you will surely be richer than any generation ever before in human history. You will live longer, be healthier, have safer, self-driving transportation, access to cheap, very high quality entertainment. and regularly eat gourmet food. As a consumer, you'll live like royalty.

In the Introduction, we mentioned *creative destruction*. It's very easy to see all the jobs that are being destroyed. We've detailed many of those in this book: lawyers, truck drivers, professors, travel agents, etc., etc. It's much harder to forecast the jobs that are being created. Who, for example, in 1960 could have predicted employment as a *medical database administrator running Oracle software*?

For every job that will be destroyed, eventually a new one will be created. People will always find ways to trade goods and services with each other. Many new career opportunities will open up for you—it's just that we have absolutely no idea what they'll be.

And *eventually* may be a long time. Folks don't invent new jobs instantly, so there may be a decade or two while the job market is out of whack. Automation will eliminate more jobs than it creates in the short run. (Then, as the old saying goes, *in the long run we'll all be dead*.) So, you may very well have to struggle for a job. You will need to be *good at what you do*.

To avail yourself of the coming cornucopia of products and opportunities, you need to have money. It is all the more important that you *Save Money Now*. Stay out of debt.

Your job may not provide much meaning or enjoyment. Though for all that it sucks, it will earn you a good living. And you won't be working that hard for it, either. But you may not be able to invest yourself in your career the way that your parents or grandparents might have. You're much less likely to "love" your job. You can no longer trust the job market to provide you with a meaningful life.

There's the hoary advice that maybe your grandfather told you: *if it's worth doing, it's worth getting paid for.* Forget that. It's not true in the New Normal.

In the New Normal, you only get paid for doing stuff that consumers can't or don't want to do for themselves. That stuff is often not much fun. We can rephrase your Grandpa's adage: *If it isn't any fun, that's when you'll get paid for it.* Or, like the small town lawyer doing the criminal law she loves, she won't get paid very much for it.

But it's still important to be passionately involved in something—if not your career, then something else.

- For some it is religion.
- Others are keen on literature—perhaps studying Shakespeare.
- Maybe you like photography and travel to exotic places.
- Sports and outdoor activities are important for many people.
- Do you like growing flowers? Or making art?

Whatever it is, while you're young you need to find that passion and cultivate it. The New Normal is bad in the sense that your job is less likely to feed your passion, but it's better in that you will have both the time and money to pursue it on your own.

Sigmund Freud wrote that

Love and work are the cornerstones of our humanness.

Love—establishing enduring relationships (typically, a family)—is an important task of early adulthood. Some of you will go to college precisely for that reason, perhaps pursuing the much maligned MRS degree. There is nothing wrong with that, though you won't find much advice in these pages. Buy another book.

The problem with the New Normal is that work becomes increasingly just about the cash. The "spiritual" aspects of work are being disaggregated away. Satisfaction and meaning will come from your passions—your hobbies—valuable work that you do for its own sake. Tom plays the piano. Dan writes books. Some people build model trains.

What will you do?

ENDNOTES

1   Data from www.bea.gov.

2   Cowen, Tyler. (2011) *The Great Stagnation: How America Ate All The Low-Hanging Fruit of Modern History, Got Sick, and Will (Eventually) Feel Better.* New York, NY: Dutton-Penguin.

3   Steadman, Ian. (2013 February 11) *IBM's Watson Is Better at Diagnosing Cancer than Human Doctors.* Retrieved from http://wired.co.uk (http://www.wired.co.uk/news/archive/2013-02/11/ibm-watson-medical-doctor)

4   The Creative Group (2015) Retrieved from http://www.roberthalf.com/creativegroup

5   The Creative Group (2011) Social Media Job Descriptions.pdf retrieved from http://www.roberthalf.com/creativegroup (http://www.roberthalf.com/creativegroup/External_Sites/downloads/TCG/tcg-us/social-media-job-description.pdf)

6   The Creative Group (2015) Moolah Paloozah.pdf retrieved from http://www.roberthalf.com/creativegroup (http://www.roberthalf.com/creativegroup/marketing-salaries)

7   Lawrencekhoo (Own work) [Public domain], via Wikimedia Commons

8   Kling, Arnold (2011) "PSST: Patterns of Sustainable Specialization and Trade," *Capitalism and Society:* Vol. 6: Iss. 2, Article 2. (http://arnoldkling.com/essays/papers/PSSTCap.pdf)

9   Steinbeck, John (1939) *The Grapes of Wrath.* New York, NY: Viking Press.

10   Brynjolfsson, Eric and Andrew McAfee (2014) *The Second Machine Age: Work, Progress and Prosperity in a Time of Brilliant Technologies.* New York, NY: W. W. Norton.

11   Boston Dynamics (2010) *Big Dog.* Youtube video. (https://youtu.be/cNZPRsrwumQ). Boston Dynamics (2013) *Wild Cat.* Youtube video. (https://youtu.be/wE3fmFTtP9g).

12   Smith, Jennifer (2013 December 13) US Law School Enrolments Fall, *Wall Street Journal*. (http://www.wsj.com/news/articles/SB10001424052702304858104579264730376317914)

13   Scheiber, Noam (2013 July 21) The Last Days of Big Law. *The New Republic*. (http://www.newrepublic.com/article/113941/big-law-firms-trouble-when-money-dries)

14   Markoff, John (2011 March 4) Armies of Expensive Lawyers, Replaced by Cheaper Software. *The New York Times*. (http://www.nytimes.com/2011/03/05/science/05legal.html?pagewanted=all&_r=0)

15   Clarey, Aaron (2011) *Worthless*. Excelsior, MN: Paric Publishing, LLC.

16   Madhani, Aamer (2014 February 19) Obama Apologizes for Joking About Art History Majors. *USA Today*. (http://www.usatoday.com/story/theoval/2014/02/19/obama-apologizes-to-texas-art-history-professor/5609089/)

17   Caplan, Bryan. *Try Harder or Do Something Easier*. 2014 April 16, blogpost. econlog.econlib.org. Retrieved 2015. (http://econlog.econlib.org/archives/2014/04/try_harder_or_g.html)

18   Lipka, Sara (2013 August 20) *A Practical College Education, Debt Free*. A podcast distributed by The Chronicle of Higher Education, http://chronicle.com/blogs. Retrieved 2015. (http://chronicle.com/blogs/saysomething/2013/08/20/a-practical-college-education-debt-free/).

19   Roberts, Russ (2014 April 7) *Bryan Caplan on College, Signaling and Human Capital*. Podcast at Econtalk.org. (http://www.econtalk.org/archives/_featuring/bryan_caplan/)

20   Scheiber, Noam (2013 July 21) The Last Days of Big Law. *The New Republic*. (http://www.newrepublic.com/article/113941/big-law-firms-trouble-when-money-dries)

21   Cowen, Tyler (2013) *Average is Over: Powering America Beyond the Age of the Great Stagnation*. New York, NY, Plume.

22   Nisen, Max (2014 February 24) Why Google Doesn't Care About Hiring Top College Graduates. *Quartz*, web qz.com. (http://qz.com/180247/why-google-doesnt-care-about-hiring-top-college-graduates/)

23   Maciag, Mike (2011 September 29) *Census: Government's Share of Workforce Varies Greatly Among States*. www.governing.

com. (http://www.governing.com/news/state/2010-census-public-employees-workforce-among-states.html)

24   United States Postal Service (2014) *A Decade of Facts and Figures*, website www.usps.com. (https://about.usps.com/who-we-are/postal-facts/decade-of-facts-and-figures.htm).

Ginsberg, W. (2008). *U.S. Postal Service workforce size and employment categories, 1987-2007* (RS22864). Washington, DC: Congressional Research Service. (http://digitalcommons.ilr.cornell.edu/key_workplace/509/)

Infoplease Encyclopedia (2011) *Active Duty Military Personnel*, 1940-2011. http://www.infoplease.com/ipa/A0004598.html

25   Tabarrok, Alex (2013 September 7) *Firefighter Hysteresis, Marginal Revolution* blog (http://marginalrevolution.com/marginal-revolution/2013/09/firefighter-hysteresis.html)

26   Williamson, Kevin (2013) *The End Is Near and It's Going to Be Awesome: How Going Broke Will Leave America Richer, Happier, and More Secure*. New York, NY: Broadside e-books.

27   *Compound Annual Growth Rate* (Annualized Return). www.moneychimp.com (http://www.moneychimp.com/features/market_cagr.htm)

28   ("*Compound Interest with Varying Frequencies*" by Jelson25 - Own work. Licensed under CC BY-SA 3.0 via Wikimedia Commons http://commons.wikimedia.org/wiki/File:Compound_Interest_with_Varying_Frequencies.svg#/media/File:Compound_Interest_with_Varying_Frequencies.svg)

29   Data taken from the US Inflation Calculator webpage: http://www.usinflationcalculator.com/inflation/consumer-price-index-and-annual-percent-changes-from-1913-to-2008/

30   Piketty, Thomas (2013) *Capital in the 21st Century*. Cambridge, MA: Harvard University Press.

31   Social Security Administration. *Period Life Table*, 2010. Webpage http://www.ssa.gov, retrieved 2015. (http://www.ssa.gov/oact/STATS/table4c6.html)

32   https://studentaid.ed.gov

33   www.payscale.com. (http://www.payscale.com/college-roi/)

34   The methodology for the ROI calculation is described at http://www.payscale.com/college-roi/methodology.

35   The median is halfway between the top and the bottom. If the schools are ranked from highest ROI (1) to lowest ROI (1,312), then the school at place 656 represents the median. A story illustrates how the median differs from the average. Nine guys are sitting in a bar. The richest guy leaves the room, and Bill Gates walks in. The average income is now much, much bigger, but the median income hasn't changed at all. It's still the salary of the guy 5th from the top.

36   Roose, Kevin (2014 February 19) The Woes of Wall Street: Why Young Bankers Are So Miserable. *The Atlantic.* (http://www.theatlantic.com/business/archive/2014/02/the-woes-of-wall-street-why-young-bankers-are-so-miserable/283927/)

37   Martin, Felix (2014) *Money: The Unauthorized Biography.* New York, NY: Knopf.

38   Roberts, Russ (2014 August 4) *Reid Hoffman and Ben Casanocha on LinkedIn and The Alliance.* Podcast from Econtalk. org. Retrieved 2015. (http://www.econtalk.org/archives/2014/08/reid_hoffman_an.html)

39   Newton, Casey (2014 June 17) *Taskrabbit Is Blowing Up its Business Model and Becoming the Uber for Everything.* The Verge website. Retrieved 2015. (http://www.theverge.com/2014/6/17/5816254/taskrabbit-blows-up-its-auction-house-to-offer-services-on-demand)

40   Said, Carolyn (2014 July 18) *Taskrabbit Makes Some Workers Hopping Mad.* SFGATE website. Retrieved 2015. (http://www.sfgate.com/technology/article/TaskRabbit-makes-some-workers-hopping-mad-5629239.php)

41   https://www.wunwun.com/faqs

42   https://www.fiverr.com

43   Danielle (2015) I will proofread and copy edit your 1000 word document for $5. www.fiverr.com. (https://www.fiverr.com/danisellis/proofread-and-edit-your-document-up-to-1500-words?context=advanced_search&context_type=rating&funnel=2014080518284877214914360)

44   Rodneywoods (2015) I will write your research paper, essay, and homework for $5. www.fiverr.com. https://www.fiverr.com/

rodneywoods/write-your-essay-assignment-research-paper-and-homework?context=adv.cat_5.subcat_107&context_type=rating&funnel=20140805183702137102203 20

45   For a photo, go to http://upload.wikimedia.org/wikipedia/commons/thumb/4/4a/Checker_A-11_Taxicab_1982.jpg/500px-Checker_A-11_Taxicab_1982.jpg

46   Whyte, William (1956) *The Organization Man*. New York, NY: William Schuster.

47   Cadillac (2014) *Cadillac Summer's Best Event TV Spot, 'Robot Arms'*. ispot.tv. (http://www.ispot.tv/ad/7lt_/cadillac-summers-best-event-robot-arms)

ABOUT THE AUTHORS

Daniel Jelski is a professor of chemistry at SUNY New Paltz, previously serving as dean of science & engineering. A native of Oregon, Dan spent part of his high school years in his father's home town, Berlin, Germany. In 1996, Dan and his family (wife Valerie and two children) spent a year in Kampala, Uganda, where he taught chemistry at Makerere University.

Thomas F. George is chancellor and professor of chemistry and physics at the University of Missouri St. Louis. He holds a BA, Phi Beta Kappa, from Gettysburg College (chemistry and mathematics) and MS and PhD degrees from Yale University (chemistry), with postdoctoral appointments at MIT and UC, Berkeley. Along with his wife, Barbara Harbach, Tom is an accomplished musician.

www.ingramcontent.com/pod-product-compliance
Lightning Source LLC
Chambersburg PA
CBHW060609200326
41521CB00007B/714